Dateline: New Mexico

Dateline:
New Mexico

Toby Smith
Foreword by Tony Hillerman

University of New Mexico Press
Albuquerque

Library of Congress Cataloging in Publication Data

Smith, Toby, 1947–
   Dateline New Mexico.

   A series of articles which originated in the Albuquerque Journal.
     1. New Mexico—Social life and customs—Addresses, essays, lectures. 2. New Mexico—Biography—Addresses, essays, lectures. I. Title.
F801.2.S63   1982   978.9'05   82–11127
ISBN 0–8263–0628–4

© 1982 by the University of New Mexico Press. All rights reserved.
Manufactured in the United States of America.
Library of Congress Catalogue Card Number 82-11127.
International Standard Book Number 0-8263-0628-4.
First edition.
Illustrations © by Greg Tucker.

The collection of articles in this book appeared originally as feature pieces in the *Albuquerque Journal*. They are reproduced in revised form with the permission of the Editor, *Albuquerque Journal*.

"I say no more of New Mexico as it is today, except that here surely is a place where many kinds of men live and work, where one may dig or dream, make poems, bricks or love, or merely sit in the sun, and find some tolerance and some companionship."
—Harvey Fergusson (from *Rio Grande)*

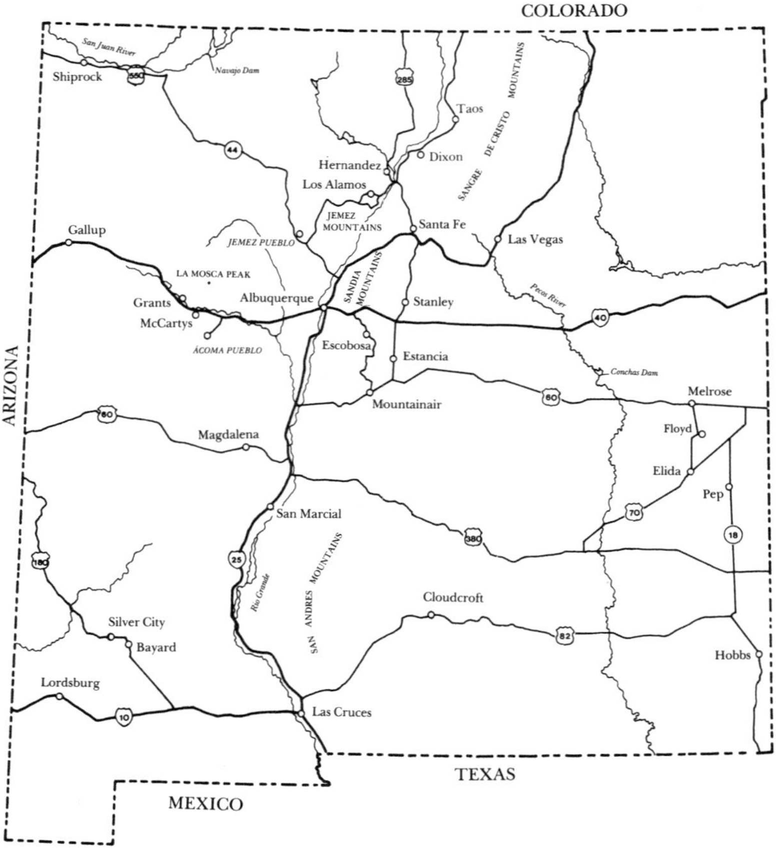
COLORADO
San Juan River
Shiprock
550
Navajo Dam
285
Taos
SANGRE DE CRISTO MOUNTAINS
44
Dixon
Hernandez
Los Alamos
JEMEZ MOUNTAINS
Santa Fe
Gallup
JEMEZ PUEBLO
Las Vegas
LA MOSCA PEAK
SANDIA MOUNTAINS
Grants
Albuquerque
Stanley
McCartys
Pecos River
40
ÁCOMA PUEBLO
Escobosa
Estancia
ARIZONA
Conchas Dam
Melrose
80
Mountainair
60
Floyd
Magdalena
Elida
Pep
San Marcial
70
18
SAN ANDRES MOUNTAINS
380
180
25
Rio Grande
Cloudcroft
Silver City
Bayard
82
Hobbs
Lordsburg
10
Las Cruces
TEXAS
MEXICO

Contents

Foreword by Tony Hillerman   ix
Preface   xi

1 Pioneers
   They Called Her Madam   3
   The Trail of History   9
   Onions   14
   Newshound   22
   On a Clear Day You Can See Shiprock   29

2 Survivors
   One-Room Master   35
   Cowboys and Religion   40
   Lovers   45
   Healer   50
   Washed Away   56

3 Achievers
   The Selling of an Artist   65
   Local Hero   77
   Urban Indian   83
   Mind Reader   88
   Shu-Pac Operator   93
   Mountain Goat   100

4 Celebrators
   The Game   109
   Picture Perfect   116
   For Sale   122
   Remembering Reagan   127
   Good Ol' Boy   133

5 Givers
   The Champ   141
   The Flight of 59816   147
   A Dad Named Eddie   153
   A Real Gas Pain   157
   Rescue in Rio Arriba County   163

6 Overcomers
   Eyewitness   173
   Wayne Wallace, Farmer   179
   The Lodger   183
   Chasing the Cure   189
   Christmas Story   195

7 Dreamers
   He Does It His Way   203
   Smitty's Bridge   209
   The Long Walk   217
   Gone Fishin'   226

Foreword
Tony Hillerman

To those who come from lusher climates, New Mexico doesn't look like a place God intended for human habitation. I think it's because of this that those of us who fall in love with the state find ourselves always trying to explain the illogical attraction. Toby Smith's way is different but effective. He introduces us to a bookful of our neighbors and, since we come to know them through the eyes and ears of an uncommonly gifted and astute reporter, we find ourselves understanding the place as well as the people who occupy it.

Obviously Renaldo Estrada, who has spent his life teaching five subjects to six grades in the one-room Conchas Dam Elementary School, would have far different stories to tell if he'd spent his life in Chicago. But that's only part of the way it works. After all, Kathleen Tohe has just moved here from Chicago. Now she spends half her years atop the fire lookout on La Mosca Peak, sharing space with the Turquoise Girl of Navajo mythology and learning to live with loneliness. Add Tohe and Estrade to Robert Saul, who checked into room 18 in the Mountainair Hotel 10,000 nights ago for a lifetime stay. The people of Mountainair call him Doctor and through Toby Smith we hear one of them say this: "When you're sick, Doctor's sick. When you cry, he cries." I don't know about that, but I can assure you that just meeting Doctor between these pages will make you feel a little better.

This makes Smith's book sound sentimental—which it isn't. There is nothing sentimental about our visit with Patti Hopper, who had the bad luck to witness a murder and the conscience to force her to behave the way we all like to think we'd behave. There is nothing sentimental about Maria Toscano, who measures life's generosity by the dimensions of the onions she's working among. There is certainly no sentiment in the portrait Toby Smith gives us of R. C. Gorman.

In fact, the R. C. Gorman to whom Smith introduces us amid the splendors of the Navajo artist's multi-million dollar Taos adobe stands as the very reverse of sentimental. We meet Gorman at his apricot tinted telephone laughing his har-de-har-har belly laugh at the art world he's beaten at its own scruffy game, and we're reminded of what the late Dr. W. W. Hill said about Navajos refining sardonic humor to an art form.

If it makes sense to name the Roadrunner the official New Mexico bird, and the piñon the official New Mexico tree, why not R. C. Gorman as the official New Mexico human? Why not? Because among the 35 portraits in Smith's gallery of New Mexicans there's a lot of competition for the title. There's Wayne Wallace, for example, a raw-boned Estancia Valley farmer calculating the odds against bankruptcy each dawn at his kitchen table, and Aloysius Waquie with his love affair with La Luz Trail, and Michael Brown who, at 13, was brave enough and wise enough to keep a dying woman alive on a rain-swept cliff.

In his poking around New Mexico, Toby Smith has found for us a people full of stories.

Preface

How clearly I remember the moment. "See what you can discover," my editor said, with deliberate vagueness, "about the people who live in New Mexico." That offhand proposal began for me a marvelous quest. What made the assignment rewarding (and I would like to think successful), was that when I started on it I knew few New Mexicans and had even fewer preconceived ideas about them. When I finished I had talked to many: the famous and unfamiliar, the overachiever and the underprivileged, the big-city dweller and the small-town inhabitant. Listening to this cross-section describe what they do, what they did, what they hoped to do, provided me with a portrait of life's joys and disappointments, as well as a sense of place.

I am often amazed at the numbers who have only been *through* this place. ("Ever been to New Mexico?" Answer: "Driven through it, on my way to California.") My first occasion to pass through came in the summer of 1951; my parents drove out in a dimpled green Chevrolet. We were coming from Connecticut, going to Arizona and I was five-years-old. Save for a faded (and hot) recollection of the

White Sands, I recall little of New Mexico, and nothing of its people.

Twenty years went by before I was through again. I was heading east this time, and it was winter. Freshly sprung from the Army, I was flying home when my plane made a brief stop in Albuquerque. From the cabin window I glimpsed an Indian. Was it safe here, I wondered?

Within five years I had moved to New Mexico. The woman I married had visited the state extensively; she showed me that staying was a lot better than passing through. She also explained to me a little about Indians.

Not long after my arrival I began working for the *Albuquerque Journal*. If you happen to be a newspaper writer who likes to travel (is there any other kind?), the *Journal* can be accommodating. It was at the *Journal* that I received my peripatetic assignment, the origin of the pieces that follow.

Searching out these profiles often meant running obstacles. In Deming, it was a snowstorm. In Carlsbad, a broken transmission. In Farmington, no vacancy. Small inconveniences when one learns that scratching a New Mexican will more than likely yield a story—educational, inspirational, historical, painful, even zany.

What then did I discover about the people who live in New Mexico? That they are as different from one another as lightning is from a lightning bug. Although most of the New Mexicans I met probably wouldn't care to be categorized, I've placed them into one of seven classifications. If there is a single thread that runs through all, it is accomplishment. For *Pioneers*, it's simply to accomplish something as a woman. For *Survivors*, it's to persevere, especially when faced with vocational modernization. *Achievers* have triumphed in large and small ways. *Celebrators* help proclaim a community's notability. *Givers* have lent assistance, and often more. *Overcomers* have reacted well to life's detours. And *Dreamers* have accomplished what they have wanted, how they have wanted.

My deepest gratitude goes to the people in this book, whatever their category. Opening a home as well as a heart is something New Mexicans do readily. I offer additional thanks to David Holtby, of the University of New Mexico Press, who edits with care; and to my wife, Susan, whose caring edifies.

1: Pioneers

"The people who came to see me, they know who they are."

They Called Her Madam

BAYARD—"Sweetheart," Milly Cusey was saying as she placed a hand with sculpted, crimson-colored fingernails atop the stranger's. "Sweetheart, you either do things in life for love or for money. I sure didn't do what I did for love." But oh, how she loved it. For thirty-three years, Mildred Clark Cusey ran some of the most profitable houses of ill repute this side of the Place Pigale. Working for the classiest madam in southwestern New Mexico, Milly's girls were the busiest bodies in town. Around these parts, her houses are still mournfully referred to by some wags as "The Last of the Red Hot Covers."

It was more than ten years ago that Milly Cusey allegedly gave up managing the backside of life. And now, after a decade of dormancy, she was fixing to sell a warehouse full of items from her famed brothels. On this day, Milly was shuttling among a Bayard storeroom where a tag sale of her earthly possessions was being held; her mobile home in nearby Central; and the place where she earned her biggest reputation—Silver City.

When Milly, now an ivory-haired sixty-six, has a few

moments to talk, the conversation naturally turns to her old line of work. "I don't regret anything I did, honey. The hardest thing I've ever done was to stand and watch all my houses be torn down in Silver and see that post office be built where they were. A man once told me he didn't need the mail half as much as he needed me."

Milly has an endearing way of laughing about her career of caresses, and during the tag sale, where nearly 5,000 pieces of bordello-ware were being peddled—from steamer trunks to mattresses—Milly laughed a lot. Curiously, one had the feeling that while some people were secretly relieved Milly was finally out of business, they were also pleased to discover what Milly has always been: a tough and tender lady. "The odd part of it," says Milly, "is that women as well as men like me now. Have you noticed? And the funny thing is, I was never a threat to a home. Never." As she says this, a woman with two china figurines appears. "Excuse me, Milly," the woman says shyly. "My daughter collects these things. Would you mind autographing the bottoms?"

In three decades Milly Cusey made three enemies. One was the former chief of police in Silver City, Tommy Ryan. Many in Silver feel Ryan was responsible for Milly's closing down. In court, Ryan testified as to the illegality of Milly's establishments, which had stood on Silver's Hudson Street since anyone could remember. Then Milly testified that Ryan had patronized her houses. Ryan, reportedly eager for an FBI appointment, impugned the madam's livelihood. Milly in turn made cracks about certain anatomical shortcomings of Ryan's.

The tag sale this day has Milly bubbly, but confused. "I can run a lot of things, honey, but this ain't one." She has been helped in the sale by two Hillsboro antique dealers. Dressed in a white blouse and black slacks, Milly scans the crowd. "Now, you'll notice, honey, that I don't speak to anyone unless he speaks to me. You can bet your boots that I've seen some of these people in the past." An old cowboy, with a wife in tow, walks by Milly and nods politely. "Howdy," responds Milly gaily. "Yes," she continues, "I've done business with newspaper editors, doctors, judges, county, state, and national officials. The people who came to see me, they know who they are."

Those who did visit in the good old days and nights might remember a few of the dozens and dozens of ashtrays for sale in the warehouse. There are ashtrays shaped like liquor bottles. Ashtrays shaped like outhouses. Ashtrays shaped like beds. There are broken-down chairs, rocking chairs, and signs. Milly's business was a word-of-mouth operation, but there are all kinds of signs here for sale. "Gospel Meeting in Progress," says an old white one. "Open for Business," declares another. There is an "Office" sign. There is a sign on the headboard of a bed saying "Do It," and one for the baseboard that reads, "Don't Talk About It." There are lamps of all kinds. Lamps shaped like liquor bottles. Lamps shaped like outhouses. Lamps shaped like ashtrays.

"I don't know if all this stuff was even in her houses," says an amateur antique dealer named Haskell Smith. Smith has travelled to Bayard from Las Cruces, and has his wife with him. "A lot of this stuff seems like junk," allows Smith, a seventy-year-old who has lived in New Mexico since 1934. "I always heard she kept her houses pretty well under control. Course, I was never in one of her places, you understand."

While Milly's sale goes on, ten miles away, in Silver City, a man who has known her since 1948 is sitting in a trailer and reminiscing. Ernie Brown would like to visit the sale, but says he has too much else to do. For several years, Brown, a tanned gentleman in his sixties, was mayor of Silver City, When he first came to town he ran the Silver City Cab Company. "Driving a cab I got to know Mildred real well. We used to haul her girls around to the doctor. Mildred was always insistent her girls get regular physical checkups. Every once in a while I'd deposit money in the bank for Mildred. No, I never felt uncomfortable doing it and I never knew how much it was. Could have been fifty dollars or $5,000, for all I know."

Brown feels Milly's houses were an asset to Silver City, that they kept the crime rate down and kept prostitution indoors. "Mildred would never let her girls go downtown to solicit nor could they visit bars in town. She was real strict with them." While he was mayor in the 1960s, Brown got in a disagreement with Tommy Ryan over Milly's houses. Brown supported Milly's staying, but he says now he thinks Milly had just reached the point of not wanting to be a madam anymore. "I don't think any one man or group of men could have forced her to shut down. She helped too many people in this town. Mildred was always giving to the needy. She fed all the children when we had a miners' strike here some years back. She is the most sincere person I ever met. So honest you could set your watch by her."

Lots of times when Ernie Brown was driving a cab people would ask him for directions to Milly's houses. "We never promoted her whereabouts, but her places were right down the street from here, two blocks from where the police station is now. Real fancy houses they were, too, with entertainment rooms and bars and all. Of course, I never really went inside."

Those shopping at the Bayard warehouse can hear a faint whistle in the distance. Milly looks at her wristwatch, then announces in a voice of someone who knows, "The shifts at the mines are changing. We'll have some more business here in a few minutes." As the afternoon wears on, Milly reflects on her calling. Born in Kentucky, orphaned at six, she came to Deming at fourteen to work as a Harvey House girl. When her older sister required treatment in a sanatorium, Milly helped finance the care by taking work in a Carrizozo cat house. But Milly never wanted to be a prostitute; she wanted to be the boss. By the time she was in her late twenties, Milly was running six houses: four in Silver City, one in Lordsburg, and one in Laramie, Wyoming.

Milly Cusey stories have a way of being embellished. Not the type to want to set the record *too* straight, Milly does a little adorning herself. "Now, I had a girl working for me once who had just bought a pair of high heel shoes. The day she got 'em that girl turned ninety-seven tricks. 'Aren't you tired?' I asked her. 'No,' she says, 'but my feet hurt'." Another: "Once I had a girl who was so darn dumb I told her I was going to have to start holding school. I said this one evening in front of a particular person—call him a teacher if you like. Next day there were two desks from the Sixth Street School sitting in front of my house." And another: "The highway department called me up one time and said that there were six big trees on the edge of my property that had to be cut down. I told them I didn't know how I was ever going to get the job done. I mean, I just couldn't advertise, 'Men Wanted,' could I?"

When a young couple buys up one of Milly's old bedroom tables, she is reminded of something. "You know, when we were getting ready for this sale, I opened the drawer of one old dresser and found about 500 prophylactics and a set of false teeth, upper plate. Some man had left in a hurry, wouldn't you say, honey?"

One man who has been at Milly's side for twenty-eight

years is her husband, Wendell Cusey, a leathery-looking rancher and contractor. "I never lied to Wendell about what I did and I guess that's how come we got along so good. Children? Honey, if you visited my houses on a Saturday night you'd have seen all the little girls I had."

For the past year or so Milly has been working with Albuquerque writer Max Evans on a biography. "It's been going slow," reports Evans. "The trouble with a person like Milly is that she's got too much material. It's hard to decide what to use and what not to." Says Milly: "I'm retired now, I guess, but life is never dull. The one thing I think about a lot these days is that there's so few real houses left. Only freelancing, and that gets so high-priced. I suppose that as the cost of living goes up, so does the price of hookers. I can remember during the war when my girls' prices were higher than a cat's back."

As Milly says this, a middle-aged woman leaves the warehouse. She has purchased a stack of old magazines once belonging to Milly. On the top of the pile, in the crook of the woman's arm, the cover of one magazine is visible. It is a 1954 issue and its title, perhaps more than any other possession, tells the story of Mildred Clark Cusey. The magazine is *Good Housekeeping.*

Some months after this piece appeared, I had occasion to travel back to the Silver City area. While there, I asked about Milly. "Oh, she's still operating," one gent confirmed. "But I'm not sure where."

The Trail of History

SANTA FE—Dr. Myra Ellen Jenkins likes to tell about the man who came to the Records and Archives building here to study information on a ghost town. For a couple of hours, Dr. Jenkins lugged ancient, fraying data to the gentleman until, finally, she decided to ask what, exactly, was he searching. "I'm trying to find the location of a certain well," the man replied, not looking up. Dr. Jenkins, who some say knows the whereabouts of every well in New Mexico, asked why. "Because," the man said, "I've heard there's an albino rattlesnake at the bottom of that well, and I want to capture it and sell it to a zoo."

An albino rattler isn't the sort of query Myra Ellen Jenkins normally receives, but if there's a connection to New Mexico history, she's willing to listen to almost anything. Sued for one million dollars by land grant activist Reies Lopez Tijerina, damned by Victorio Peak gold hunters, admired yet feared by every manner of scholar, Myra Ellen Jenkins, like that snake, is something of a rarity: she's the first and only state historian New Mexico has had.

Sitting in her office, her slight, stooped frame peeking

from behind a pile of discolored ledgers belonging to a dry goods firm extinct 100 years, she talked of her work, with customary dramatic flair. In voice and appearance she bears great resemblance to actress Margaret Hamilton, late of *The Wizard of Oz,* more recently seen in television coffee commercials.

"When we began here, in 1960, we were totally frustrated. New Mexico had 300 years of records and they'd never been organized. People had dumped the state's historical files, which are as rich as any state's in the country, into every kind of hidey-hole." Combing warehouses and courthouse basements, Dr. Jenkins began to fill the Records Center and Archives. It now houses several million volumes, or "cubic feet," as they call it in the archivist profession. Daily, large trucks pull up to the building's loading dock with another half ton or so of state agency paperwork to be microfilmed or recycled.

Dr. Jenkins is part of that decision—save or throw out—but she doesn't really care to administer. "I'm a historian," she says flatly. And "Dr. J," as her staff calls her, takes her history seriously. She is not afraid to jump feet first on misinformation or trounce on myths. She isn't, however, some picky drudge who delights in finding fault; she holds her adopted state's past as sacred as a child might a stuffed animal.

Has she ever been proved wrong? "Oh, Lord, yes," she says. "And I'm always the first to admit it." Few people can remember even fewer times when Myra Ellen Jenkins had to admit to any mistake. Not surprisingly, Dr. Jenkins's knowledge is in demand. Church groups, library societies, and Moose lodges are eager to hear her speak. "She's got a photographic memory," says a Records and Archives worker. "What you don't know about New Mexico, Dr. J will be happy to tell you."

Her desktop correspondence confirms this. A young man from Los Angeles wants information about some relatives. "They're Hispano," says Dr. Jenkins. "He's got a good chance of finding out." A woman in Colorado has sent a map she believes is of great value. "It's a fantasy map," Dr. Jenkins snaps, tossing the paper down. She holds up a historical article someone has mailed her. "The research is good, but whoever did this map is cuckoo."

Maps—charts of ancient land grants piled upon one another like stacks of flapjacks; tattered maps of labyrinth-like town plazas; Spanish explorers' maps with more watermarks than detail—are a Jenkins's love. "If I could," she sighs, "I'd wallpaper every room in my house with maps."

There aren't many maps in her celebrated *A Brief History of New Mexico*, coauthored with Albert Schroeder, but the slim book is one of the widest-read pieces of literature on the state. No one knows for sure whether Reies Lopez Tijerina ever read *A Brief History*, but Tijerina knows one of its authors well. Jenkins once suggested privately that Tijerina might be involved in a "con" game in his militant land grant claims (which eventually led to the infamous Tierra Amarilla courthouse raid in 1967 and a subsequent prison sentence), to which Tijerina responded by slapping the state historian with a whopping lawsuit, later dismissed.

It's unlikely that greater opposites have been attracted: big, gruff Reies Tijerina; bookish, bird-like Myra Ellen Jenkins. Yet the two have actually become friends; since his release from prison, Tijerina shows up periodically at the Records and Archives, apparently still searching out obscure title claims. Says Dr. Jenkins: "We've decided to agree on what we don't agree on."

Authenticity is something Dr. Jenkins never has trouble agreeing on. Some years ago a woman from Pennsylvania came to her office with a folder of historically important

Spanish documents the woman had discovered in an attic. How the seventeenth century papers, missing for 100 years, found their way to Pennsylvania, Dr. Jenkins can only surmise. But seeing them made her gasp. ("I almost lost my teeth.") An offer was made and the woman handed over the documents. "Obtaining something like that," Dr. Jenkins says, "isn't completed until you get your hot little hands on the material and get it into a vault."

A Jenkins theory is that people don't destroy records. "They steal them, sit on them, but they don't usually get rid of them." When a batch of Spanish records was traced to a Kansas City book dealer, Dr. Jenkins's office took the dealer to court. New Mexico lost the case, but the stern and righteous presence of Dr. J in court set down a precedent: keep your hands off official New Mexico papers or you'll be in trouble.

Two documents that have never been found nag at her sense of order. One was the emotional surrender speech of Juan Bautista Vigil y Alarid, in Santa Fe in 1846. The other, a 1748 report detailing an Indian massacre in Abiquiu. People who do claim genuine articles are in for tough scrutiny. A couple once came to Dr. Jenkins with a rawhide map they said led to gold mines in southwestern New Mexico. The man and wife wanted Dr. Jenkins to accompany them on their search for that gold, and offered her all sorts of money to go. It wasn't so much the money that made Dr. Jenkins refuse. It was, she says, the fact that the map's trail had been engraved with a child's woodburning tool.

A few years ago, when swarms with the scent of buried treasure in their nostrils circled Victorio Peak, in southern New Mexico, Dr. Jenkins went down for a look. She knew there was as much chance of finding old "Doc" Noss's gold stash as there was of finding whales in Elephant Butte

Lake. Calling the treasure claims "historical nonsense," she became, she says, the "least popular person in the whole White Sands."

The daughter of a Colorado rancher who had a third-grade education, Myra Ellen Jenkins as a child was put on history's trail through a six-volume set of history books her grandfather had brought over from England. After taking bachelor's and master's degrees in history at the University of Colorado, she taught high school in that state for a few years, and frequently vacationed in New Mexico. Magnetized by New Mexico's Spanish and Mexican heritage, she came to Albuquerque after World War II to work on a doctorate at the University of New Mexico. She was freelancing in land grants and Indian water rights when the call came from Santa Fe.

At sixty-two, her energy and enthusiasm would seem to be as charged as when she began. Richard Salazar, an assistant, says, "Dr. J's not afraid to get down on her hands and knees in the dust and dirt to look for records." Never married, Dr. Jenkins is often found at her office on days off and weekends. "This is her life," says Salazar. Myra Ellen Jenkins explains her dedication this way: "I'm a historian."

Following a bureaucratic shakeup in state government, Dr. Jenkins is now self-employed. She does special research assignments—in New Mexico history, naturally—for Indian pueblos and other private groups.

Onions

LAS CRUCES—There is an expression among migrant laborers that says when work is not good in one place it is bound to be better "up the road." "Up the road," Maria Toscano muses as she wipes a forehead that glistens like glazed terra-cotta. "Up the road are the big onions." Maria Toscano picks onions for a living. She "tops" them. Onion toppers have their own expression: when people stand idle in the fields, the onions are too small. Nobody makes money. This morning there are a lot of toppers standing around Maria Toscano. *"Cebollitos,"* she explains, bending down. "Small onions." They are bound to be bigger up the road.

Although New Mexico produces only about five percent of this country's onions, at certain times of the summer the states provides nearly one-third of the nation's crop. There are onion farms in the Hatch and Uvas valleys in northern Dona Ana County. There are some onions on the east side of the state and some in Bernalillo County. But the main onion industry is located in the Mesilla Valley, in and around Las Cruces.

June through September are the busiest months, a harvest period that fills the fields with toppers. Much of the help comes from locals. Other hands are illegal aliens. The remainder, like Maria Toscano, are migrants. There are approximately five million migrant workers in the United States. The New Mexico Employment Security Commission, which closely monitors farm labor here, estimates this state has only 600 migrants. Migrant families, complete contingents of father-mother-children workers, are an even rarer sight in New Mexico. Maria Toscano's family is one. They are onion people.

This day started at 6:00 A.M. for Maria. She was up at that hour to prepare breakfast for her husband and five children in the small house they rent in east Las Cruces. By 7:00 A.M. she was working a five-acre spread in San Ysidro, a village just north of Las Cruces. At 10:00 A.M. it is ninety degrees in San Ysidro; by noon it will be ninety-eight. It will be 103 and time to quit at 1:00 P.M. It will be too hot to work.

Crouched alongside Maria is her daughter, Mary Jane, twenty-two. Mary Jane is the only family member besides her mother who still tops onions. Maria's husband, Frank, forty-eight, drives an onion truck from the fields to a Las Cruces process plant where the vegetable is graded and shipped. Three sons, Fernando, Fermin, and Fabian, load onion trucks. The Toscanos have been in Las Cruces since late May. They arrived here from the "other valley," the lower Rio Grande Valley of Texas. A large portion of the onions grown in the United States comes from the lower Rio Grande area. The rest comes mainly from California, Arizona, Colorado, and New York.

In Texas, the Toscanos rent in McAllen or Westlaco from February until the New Mexico harvest begins. The remainder of the year—September through February—

they live in Muleshoe, Texas, twenty-two miles southeast of Clovis.

One hears many stories of migrant labor abuse and plight. For the most part, the Toscanos cannot relate to those stories. Certainly they are not well-off; last year their combined wages totaled less than $9,000. But they are content, reasonably happy even, and used to the transient lifestyle. It is, however, a lifestyle that threatens to change.

Topping onions, like all stoop labor, appears easier than it is. With one hand, a laborer grabs half a dozen onions recently loosened from the earth by a tractor. Using clippers in the other hand, the topper snips off tiny roots and then, in a quick motion, removes the green stalks. Decapitated onion bulbs end up in a plastic bucket about the size of an office wastebasket. When the bucket is full, the topper dumps the contents into a burlap sack. Two buckets make one fifty-pound sack. For every sack, a topper is paid from forty-five to sixty cents, depending on the market.

"Since I'm not so tall, I don't have to bend over so much," Maria says. "When you're not so tall your back doesn't hurt." At five-feet one inch, Maria Toscano weighs about 105 pounds. She is dressed this day in an oversized khaki-colored shirt, baggy purple slacks, and tennis shoes without laces. On her head is a straw hat adorned with faded artificial flowers. It would seem nobody in his right mind would top onions hatless; yet Maria Toscano, who has been topping most of her forty-six years, did not start wearing a hat until she was forty. She tells you this not hinting she is loco; rather, she admits it to show you how durable she is. Oddly, her skin does not reveal the effects of four decades under a scorching sun. Her face is burned, yes, but remarkably uncreased. She is an attractive woman. Her hair, black as asphalt, has a spun smoothness to it.

Mary Jane Toscano greatly resembles her mother but for one thing: she does not like to eat onions. When Mary Jane goes into a restaurant, she requests that none of her food be spiced with the herb of the genus *Allium*. Both mother and daughter are fast toppers, the edge going to Maria. She is deceptively quick. Just as her gloved hand sorts through the onions in a knowing sweep, her right hand deftly removes the ends. It is continuous action; there is no wasted effort. When Maria does stop, it is to clear perspiration from her face, to sip water, or to sharpen her clippers.

"You think I am fast?" she asks. "You should have seen my Frank Jr. One hundred and fifty-three sacks is my record for one day. When the onions are big, like they are up the road, Frank Jr. one day made 200." When Maria talks of Frank Jr. it is with a certain sadness. He is the only one of her children not with her in Las Cruces. Married and the father of three, he now works on a farm in Littlefield, Texas, near Muleshoe. He is no longer a *migrante*. At some future point, very soon perhaps, Maria's other children will do like Frank Jr.: quit the fields to settle in one place. When she gets married later this year, Mary Jane will live in Clovis where her fiancé is in construction. Fernando, twenty-three, has a job waiting for him in a Muleshoe maintenance shop. Fermin, twenty, wants employment in a grain elevator there. And Fabian, nineteen, plans to be a policeman.

Frank Toscano Sr. is an affable man with a huge stomach. He speaks almost no English. Like his wife, he was born in Mathis, Texas, outside of Corpus Christi. And like Maria, he grew up a *migrante*. The two met thirty years ago near Tahoka, Texas, south of Lubbock. Maria's middle name is Guadalupe and Frank calls her "Lupe." The Toscanos have been married twenty-six years. "A good marriage," Maria says. "No complaints." What helps, she believes, is that they both work onions.

Maria is used to the hard work. She draws tremendous respect if for no other reason than because she is still in the fields. After all, Frank Sr. hasn't topped an onion in years. The Toscano sons don't care to do it anymore. Yet all admire someone who does. As a child, Maria picked vegetables and cotton. She was the oldest of seventeen children, the only girl. "I had to help my Daddy. I worked harder than some of my brothers. Once I chopped 1,300 pounds of cotton one day. My Mama said I was always different than my brothers. They got tired. I never did."

By the time she met Frank Toscano, Maria *had* gotten tired—of cotton. Onions suited her more. There was something about their pungent odor she liked. Frank Toscano also comes from a large household: he is one of eight children. Somewhere, in some generation past—and Frank isn't exactly sure which one—a relative of his came to this country from Italy. Thus the Italian surname.

During the early years of their marriage, the Toscanos lived wherever there were onions: Nampa, Idaho; Ogden, Utah. Mary Jane was born in Rocky Ford, Colorado; Fabian in Las Cruces. In 1961, the couple heard about some work in Muleshoe and went there.

When they head to Las Cruces in the late spring their belongings (and optimism) are stacked as high as Steinbeck's Joads. They come by caravan: Maria and Mary Jane in the pickup, Frank in his big onion truck, the boys in an old car they've picked up en route. In Las Cruces they are welcomed by Frank Villarreal, who runs Griffin and Brand, a principal packer and harvester of onions.

Maria calls Villarreal "Chico." She has known him since the early 1950s when she came to New Mexico with her parents and brothers. "Chico is the best," Maria states. "He always looks after us, finds us work. He gets us a place to stay." The Toscanos have never known what life in a migrant labor camp is like. Maria can remember coming to New Mexico as a little girl and having it rough, but that was long ago. "When I first am here we shared a house with four families. No privacy. We had to bring everything with us—stove, lamp. No beds. My Daddy made beds and tables from wood. Mama used to carry a big tub for us to take a bath. Everything is changed now."

The only inconvenience the Toscanos experience comes during their first days in Las Cruces. They must sleep outside on the grounds of Griffin and Brand until Chico Villarreal locates decent housing for them. This year, Chico has found them an orange-stucco home in a pleasant neighborhood. It rents for $200 a month. Villarreal pays half. In September, Villarreal throws a barbecue for everyone who has worked for him during the summer. There is a pig roast, homemade biscuits, a mariachi band.

This may be the last year the Toscanos, or most of them, attend one of Chico Villarreal's bashes. Maria's husband doesn't want her in the fields anymore. "He wants me to stay home, clean house." It would be easy for Maria to do this but she doesn't want to. Her immense pride stops her; she loves the fields. During the cold months in Muleshoe, the Toscanos mostly wait for when it's time to leave for the valley. Although Maria has a job in a Muleshoe nursing home, she says she can find no work that gives her the gratification of the harvest.

Maria speaks vaguely of going to nursing school. Only Fernando of her children has gone beyond high school— two months to South Plains College in Levelland, Texas, before he quit to his mother's distress. She has only a second grade education, and Maria would like her children to get ahead. At the same time, she wants her family with her, as she's always known it. "It can't be that way," Fernando argues. "Young people like me and my brothers, we want other jobs. Doing that was okay for my parents. They're different, you know? We don't want to move around so much as we get older."

There is talk of a mechanical onion harvester coming to the Mesilla Valley. Fields in Arizona already have them. Naturally, it worries the migrants. There are other fears. Even though New Mexico growers planted nearly 4,000 acres of onions this year and expect to do ten million dollars worth of business, onions present a risk for everyone, especially the migrant. If a spring is cool, as it was this year, an onion bulb will be small. A small bulb means one must top more onions to fill a bucket, more onions to fill a sack. Loaders won't have as much to do, nor will drivers; nobody makes money in such times.

The migrant can be hurt in other ways. Disease or sandstorm can ruin an onion crop quickly, and lay off workers. Last year, a massive truckers' strike crippled the business for several weeks. Then there is the problem of wetbacks. More and more illegal aliens are showing up at growers' fields, ready and willing to take work away from legitimate laborers.

Still, the Toscanos keep at it. Chico Villarreal says they are very special onion people. "I see less and less migrant families. If you have people in a family doing the work, then you can make some money, pool resources. But if the sons or daughters get married or leave, and only two parents work, then it's harder to make out. As far as I know, the Toscanos are the only family here, and they make it work."

Five hours beneath the Las Cruces sun has formed salt marks on Maria Toscano's jawline. Her eyes are hooded in exhaustion. Rising, she mops her chin and says: "Last year we get forty-five cents a sack. This year they promise us fifty cents, more for bigger onions. But it's back to forty-five. This work is hard. It's so hot. When the onions are small, you can't do anything. I don't mind. Up the road it will be better."

Newshound

HOBBS—Someone once declared that a small-town newspaper editor should have the nose of a bloodhound and the thick skin of an elephant. Agnes Kastner Head looks neither like a canine nor a pachyderm. Rather, she resembles a mischievous librarian. Last month, after three decades of sniffing where she was told not to, and occasionally taking licks for it, Agnes Head, editor and publisher of the weekly *Hobbs Flare,* sold her newspaper. It is an event that should not go unnoticed because Agnes Kastner Head brought to Hobbs, New Mexico, what William Allen White delivered to Emporia, Kansas: a common sense kind of journalism.

A weekly newspaper in a town of 26,000 citizens, a town already claiming a venerable daily paper, would seem an unpromising idea. Agnes Head has always liked challenges, controversy, and Republican politics. Selling the *Flare* does not completely mean relinquishing it, however. Like an anxious parent, these days Mrs. Head, seventy-four, can frequently be found at the *Flare* office, located around the corner from the Reno Club and next door to Hobbs

Plumbing. Mrs. Head presents an interesting study in contrast with the new owner-editor. Robert E. Cates is a former journalism professor at New Mexico State University. Holder of a doctorate, he is a "communications" expert. Agnes Head never took a journalism course in her life. "We have different styles," says Cates, a polite man with a bushy handlebar moustache. "I may back different candidates and issues, but I don't see our viewpoints differing that much."

Reports have it that Cates purchased the *Flare* for more than twice the yearly salary of the President of this country. That's a considerable sum to pay for a publication that is dotted with articles on white elephant sales and honor roll inductees. But the *Flare* is more than that and Robert Cates knows it. "It's personal journalism at its best," he says. "I used to teach a course in journalism history. We talked about the *Flare*. It's famous."

"The *Flare* has been a stabilizing factor here," says Bob Summers, publisher of the rival *Hobbs News-Sun*, and a man who has had his ups and downs with Agnes Head in the thirty-five years they've known each other. "She's dedicated, all right. She's had a negative attitude on things I wouldn't agree with, but she's been good for Hobbs."

Conservative battler for causes, puller of no punches, part H. L. Mencken, part I. F. Stone, Agnes Head arrived in Hobbs in March of 1930. She and her husband, J. C., came from Texas where J. C. was in the building business. They had met in El Dorado, Arkansas, where Agnes scored her first scoop by writing a piece for the local paper, complete with interior descriptions, on the opening of a new whorehouse. "When she came to Arkansas, she brought her father with her to recuperate at the hot springs," says J. C., retired now from building, as well as real estate, architeture, furniture, and hardware. "She brought her father in on a stretcher and he left walking. I knew that was the girl for me."

The oil boom had only recently begun in Hobbs when the Heads arrived. The town still was pretty raw. "Like a lot of folks here, we lived in a tent at first," Agnes says. "There was no paved streets, no water, no electricity." For the first fifteen years the Heads were in New Mexico, Agnes concentrated on raising a family—a son and two daughters. None of them, including nine grandchildren, has even been interested in journalism; this saddens her.

Soon Agnes and J. C. built a house in Hobbs. Like a *Flare* editorial, the Head home is not easily forgotten. It's a fourteen-room mansion, complete with Roman columns and mulberry trees in front, and crop rows out back. It's a curious Tara lookalike, better yet, a San Simeon set down on the Southwest plains. Fighting for space inside the house are Agnes's sprawling china collection, J. C.'s target-shooting ribbons, and stacks and stacks and stacks of yellowed *Flare*s. We used to have servants all about," sniffs J. C. "Now we have but two part-timers."

"We wanted a big house and since J. C. was from Louisiana, we wanted one like this," says Agnes, smoothing her silver hair. "Everybody—roughnecks, toolhands, all the people who owed me—helped us build this house," says J. C., mostly mild-mannered, like his wife of fifty-four years, and like Agnes, an irascible individualist.

When she owned and operated the *Flare*, Agnes would get up at 6:00 A.M. each day, fix herself a cup of coffee, sit down at her dining room table and type stories. One feature would be her celebrated front-page column, "Via the Grapevine," a combination of gossip, indignation, and country-smoked chit-chat. "I'm going to miss the writing most of all," Agnes says. "The *Flare* has been like a child to me. You almost have to own a newspaper to love it like that. As a young girl growing up in Cape Girardeau, Missouri, the first thing I ever reported on was twin calves being born. I was five-years-old. I've been writing off and on since."

In 1944, Agnes purchased the *Lovington Leader* and ran it until 1958 when she sold out. Hobbs, she says, was her city and she wanted to give all her time to a Hobbs paper. In 1948, she had started the *Flare,* a paper that takes its title from oil field torches, but which ironically also means to "burn with an unsteady light."

Things were shaky indeed that first year. "My press was sabotaged, a strike was called on me, advertisers boycotted me, and I was arrested for libel." But Agnes was determined to let nothing extinguish her fiery *Flare.* After she got all the sand out of the gears of her press, she halted the strike by chasing the strike leader out the door with a galley tray. She intimidated advertisers with antitrust action, and she got the libel suit dismissed. Four years earlier, as publisher of the *Lovington Leader,* Agnes was sued by a sheriff for making disparaging remarks about how bootlegging wasn't being cleaned up. In a carnivallike trial still talked about in Lea County, Agnes Head carted into the courtroom as evidence a case of illegal liquor she had obtained herself. She was eventually fined.

For eight years the *Flare* lost money, but thanks to J. C.'s business ventures and the *Lovington Leader* (always a money-maker) the show, the lawsuits, the allegations, the investigations, and the uncoverings went on. "I've been at odds with the Democratic party ever since I started," Agnes says. "Liberals are just too free with the public's money; they don't encourage thrift in anything. That's how come we have such a big welfare state."

Welfare has always been an itch Agnes Head has not hesitated to scratch. Once, she achieved national notoriety, along with a bevy of threats, by publishing a list of everyone in the area receiving welfare. "I think we should publish welfare rolls everywhere," she argues. "You'd be surprised at the people you can find getting food stamps. And once they get them, they've got life made."

Of all Agnes Head's targets—of hospital funds for the indigent, of closed public meetings, of the Gas Company of Hobbs, of her detailed cataloguing of local bankruptcies and divorces ("We try not to leave anybody out"), of her probing pieces the *News-Sun* wouldn't touch, like the sacred Hobbs High School basketball team (a *Flare* story earlier this year revealed why a star player was kicked off the team: burglary)—of all of this she is most proud of the role she played in saving a single, little Hobbs schoolhouse. The school was about to be torn down by a city that claimed the place's roof needed repairing. Following a volley of incensed articles in the *Flare,* the wrecker's ball was staved off and the building is now a senior citizens center. "The city said the roof leaked," Agnes scoffs. "You know something, that was eight years ago and a drop of water has yet to come through."

Except for backshop help, Agnes has been the *Flare.* A local observer says that the daily *News-Sun,* with fourteen full-time reporters, has been beaten on more stories by Agnes Head than it cares to admit. Occasionally, Agnes was aided by a summer intern, many of whom (like iconoclastic Texas writer Larry L. King, author of *The Best Little Whorehouse in Texas* have gone on to bigger things. Nearly all term their stay with the *Flare* invaluable. "It was a whole course in libel law for me," remembers one intern, who also recalls another side of Agnes Head. "She's always been against the Establishment, but one time we had a police report say that a beleaguered state official's son had been picked up for drunken driving. Mrs. Head, who normally would have swooped down on that story like a ravenous hen, decided to kill it. The family had had enough hard times, she said."

"I've printed very few retractions," says Agnes, a teetotaling lemonade lover who admits she has lousy times at state press functions. "I've made mistakes and there's probably been some things I should have left out of the paper. But years ago my father would never let me use these words: 'I'm sorry'."

The other day as she sat in the *Flare* office and watched the new owner talk business on the telephone, Agnes Head did her best to try not to listen in. "She's sold the paper, but I don't think she'll ever divorce herself from it," says Bob Summers. Several times in the past few years Agnes tried to sell the *Flare*. Before Robert Cates came along she had turned down a number of offers—"from people who would have ruined it." Once, ten years ago, she sold the *Flare* to some Texas oil men. "I didn't know it at the time, but they wanted the paper as a tax write-off. They also weren't saying anything in print about the new sales tax here and I didn't like that, either. So I just took the *Flare* right back."

A recent issue of the *Flare* seemed to show little change. A closer look, however, revealed something missing, at least temporarily: biting stories, the kind for instance Agnes wrote in her final issue under the headline, "Rip-Offs at the Cash Register Widespread."

"Mr. Cates is a smart fellow and capable, but he doesn't know the sources here in Hobbs yet," Agnes was saying as she nervously fingered the neckchain which holds her eyeglasses. "Why, just the other day I was out at an antique shop and a call girl came in and bought two china dolls for $100 cash. The girl had a fist full of money and said out loud, 'Last night was a good night.' Nobody, not even the police, is doing anything about that kind of problem anymore. The corruption, the gambling, they're still here. Used to be we'd take those people to the state line six miles away and tell them to git. Yes indeedy, Hobbs is a reporter's paradise."

A year and a half after she sold it, irrepressible Agnes Head bought back the Hobbs Flare. *"I'm really too old to be running the paper," she explained to me over the telephone. "It's just that if I don't do something, I'll wilt like a carnation."*

On a Clear Day You Can See Shiprock

GRANTS—Last year at this time Kathleen Tohe was delivering mail in Albuquerque. She is still working alone—through sleet and snow—but now she radios messages from atop a fire tower here. Since the beginning of May, shortly after the twenty-five-year-old Mrs. Tohe quit her job with the post office, she has been a lookout on La Mosca, an 11,036-foot peak that sits catty-corner from Mt. Taylor. She watches approximately 300,000 acres. It's wild country, where deer, elk, and stray cattle roam, land that is steeped in Navajo lore. There's not a mailbox within miles.

Mrs. Tohe *(Tow-hee)* had worked briefly for the Forest Service five years ago, then quit to become a letter carrier. Tired of pounding sidewalks, she reapplied to the Forest Service and was given spot duty on Sandia Crest. When the Grants job opened, she grabbed it. "I really got lucky. Seasonal jobs are hard to come by. All my friends said I was crazy to leave the security of the post office, but now every time I go to Albuquerque the traffic and everything just freaks me out."

Five days a week, from 10:00 A.M. to 7:00 P.M., Kathleen

must remain in a twelve-by-twelve foot room, ten feet off the ground, an hour's drive up a horrifyingly hilly road from Grants, in the Mt. Taylor Ranger District of the Cibola National Forest. A visitor asks, How does Mr. Tohe like his wife away from their Albuquerque home five and one-half months of the year? "Robert's pretty patient," says Kathleen of her husband, a Navajo who works for the New Indian Youth Council in Albuquerque. "He said, 'Whatever makes you happy' when we talked about it. He wants me to learn more about myself and I'm grateful for that."

Not only is Kathleen, a Chicago native, learning how to cope in the wilderness, but she is learning about the wilderness. When she isn't on duty, she reads books on geology, biology, and the history of the area. "Every rock here's got a story behind it. This is a sacred mountain to the Navajos. I'm honored to be up here."

Becoming acquainted with the terrain has been an education—and a must. "I've really got to know the landmarks; if I call in a wrong position and a fire-fighting team comes in, there's going to be some people mad at me."

To break the solitude, she listens to FM radio a lot, or spends time weaving a rug on a large loom she hauled up the mountain. Weaving is a skill passed along to her by her mother-in-law. Kathleen does Yoga, too, reads the latest *Rolling Stone,* and some *I Ching.* Yes, she plays solitaire. Days off are for Robert in Albuquerque. She'll also take in some movies and catch up on the Sunday comics. Robert makes frequent trips to La Mosca, so it's never overwhelmingly lonely. "On weekends, it's like a parade up here," she says. "When the mines close, all of Grants comes up, asking questions." Not long ago some sightseers from Albuquerque appeared at the tower and—holy smoke!—it turned out they lived right on Kathleen's old mail route.

A day begins at 6:00 A.M. or earlier. "Not having any

curtains in the tower, I have no trouble waking up. Walking out on the catwalk surrounding her tower, Kathleen will sip some orange juice. "It's 'Hello, world' time then. Just a great feeling." Then, in the crisp morning air she'll take a hike, climb about the craggy La Mosca summit. One recent dawn she spotted a golden eagle. On a clear day she can see Shiprock.

By 10:00 A.M. she is perched on a high seat in the tower, binoculars in hand, scouring the horizon. "After a while, you get to know what looks normal and what doesn't." Every hour she logs in a weather reading. While it has been getting warmer up on La Mosca, the weather has been unpredictable. Several times in May, Kathleen's thermometer dipped below freezing. She's experienced springtime blizzards, and one night an ice storm thumped her concrete tower for hours. Come July, the famous La Mosca flies will appear. La Mosca means *the fly* in Spanish, and the big summertime critters have been called by some "western New Mexico's Air National Guard."

Although she has no telephone, Kathleen does have a two-way radio and is in constant communication with the district ranger's office. Just before quitting at 7:00 P.M., she signs off to take dinner—perhaps some homegrown alfalfa sprouts, maybe a little soybean curd. "I notice I eat a whole lot less up here. Maybe it has something to do with not having a husband around asking, 'What's for dinner?'" She does have junk food urges, she says, and satisfies them on occasional trips to Grants. She also goes down the mountain for a shower at the Ranger Station. "It's really amazing how little you need up here." Kathleen shows a visitor her mainstays: a small stove, a refrigerator, a propane heater. Water is drawn from a five gallon container the Forest Service, or she, brings up.

While Kathleen hasn't spotted any substantial fires as

yet, she knows August will be her busy period, a time when she'll call in most of her 1073s (fire alerts) on the radio. Seventy-five per cent of the fires in the Cibola National Forest are started by lightning. The rest are caused by the people Smokey the Bear lectures: you and me. Before taking over her post, Kathleen received two weeks of intensive training in fire behavior, first aid, safety—instruction in just about everything except how to enjoy being alone. "I'm still going through 'hermit-titis.' Actually, I like being alone. It's not that I hate people . . . I think it does any person good to be alone. Makes you strong."

A seasonal Forest Service employee, Kathleen earns $3.56 an hour. She will be in the Grants tower until mid-October. After that she will head back to Albuquerque to take some courses at the University of New Mexico, where she is a biology major. "One of these days I'll get a degree." With that degree she hopes to go into Forest Service work full-time, or at least put in another year where she is. "I think they like the job I'm doing; nobody's said anything." Perhaps no one has complained because Kathleen is not a special case. Of forty-five Forest Service lookout towers in New Mexico, thirty-four are currently manned by women.

As grand as the Walden-like atmosphere may be, Kathleen Tohe does have one regret, one little annoyance that comes, one supposes, with the territory. From the bottom step of her tower, it is some 300 boulder-strewn yards downhill to a bathroom—the only bathroom for miles around. A few times Kathleen has tried to negotiate this passage in the dark. Not anymore. Like loneliness, it's become a hardship she's learned how to handle. "I just don't drink anything," she says, "after 5:00 P.M."

2: Survivors

"I don't know beans from buttons about other places. I only know here."

One-Room Master

CONCHAS DAM—This gigantic wall of masonry imparts a sense of permanency. A few hundred yards south, in a little crudely-built house, rests a feeling of uncertainty. "I'm running out of pupils," Reynaldo Estrada, sixty, was saying as he passed out spelling tests at the Conchas Dam Elementary School. "I don't think this school will be here much longer."

Such dark forecasts are normally not part of Rey Estrada's personality. Usually he is as upbeat as a baby's smile. But he is also wise. Conchas Dam School is one of the last one-room, one-teacher schools in New Mexico. But with twelve students, it is fading fast. If his school consolidates, a death notice to all one-roomers, Rey Estrada vows he will stay till the end. "It's all I really know," says Estrada, who walks through his classroom with the rolling gait of a sailor—which he was in World War II.

School begins at Conchas at 9:00 A.M. with the raising of the American flag. There are no bells here; just a tarnished cow clanger Estrada shakes. The day ends at 3:30 P.M. Yes, students still clap out erasers on the walk outside.

But no, a potbellied stove is not in the center of this white, cinder block schoolhouse; portable gas heaters provide the warmth.

Does this amiable and dignified man know he is a practitioner of a dying craft in New Mexico: one-room schoolhouse teaching? *"Jiminy,"* says Estrada. "I don't know beans from buttons about other places. I only know here." Here he knows well, so well he rarely relies on a lesson plan. *"Jiminy.* You got five subjects and six grades. That's thirty classes in all. Who can teach thirty classes every day? You either know this or you don't."

Proof of the success Estrada has had comes without urging. He pulls out his students' achievement test results. "Now look here," he says, pointing to a sixth grader who has scored in the eighth or ninth grade in all subjects. "I'll tell you, when my kids make the honor roll at Tucumcari (where they go on to middle school and high school) *jiminy,* that makes me proud." He's tickled too when former students go into education. Connie Lucero, he reports, is teaching in West Las Vegas, so is Rosie Gutierrez. Ruben Lucero is a guidance counselor at Espanola.

Estrada works a one-roomer the way a teacher must: in groups. As a handful of students reads *Winnie-the-Pooh* to him at a corner table, another group memorizes the continents of the world, or prepares for a spelling test. "Mr. Estrada is tough on spelling," offers Doug Murphy, a sixth grader. "He's tough 'cause he's always giving tests."

Deportment has never been a problem in a Rey Estrada classroom. "The kids here know how to behave," says their teacher. "They have good parents." In this part of the country there is no such thing as being kept after school, anyway. By 3:29 P.M., parents are lined up in the school's parking lot. Their offspring had better be along any minute—there are chores to be done. For the children who live on ranches, like Teresa Martinez, it is a long trip. Teresa's home is a thirty-minute drive, much of that over bad roads. "If I were to leave here at four o'clock," says eleven-year-old Teresa, "and open and close all the gates (for cattle) it would be nearly dark when I got there." Who can do chores in the dark? Estrada, too, knows about such work. A small, neat man with immaculate fingernails, he has chores to do nightly on his own ranch.

Should discipline be needed, Estrada handles it his way. "I'm not mean, but I'm firm. If a student doesn't finish his work, then he must do it on his own time." One's own time means not doing it at home, but rather during lunch hour or free time. Anyone who has played recess baseball with Reynaldo Estrada ("He always pitches; he lets us hit," says Tommy Gonzales) doesn't want to be cooped up inside practicing longhand or multiplication tables.

Estrada says he hasn't changed his teaching methods since he started out at eighteen. Born in the nearby village of Garita, in the ranch house where he still lives, Rey Estrada has been in the Canadian River Valley all his life. Up until the eighth grade he went to Garita School, another one-roomer that didn't last. His teacher there was Ernest Wildenstein. While still a freshman at New Mexico Highlands University, Estrada began his trade down the road at Trementina School. His own younger brothers and sisters were his students in those days. After military service in the Pacific, he returned to Trementina where he taught for twenty-three years. In 1965 Estrada was sent to Conchas.

"You got to go with the basics," he says, crediting Ernest Wildenstein for that advice. "You don't divide before you multiply, you don't add before you know combinations of numbers. This new math, *jiminy*. It's just a lot of garbage." A good teacher, says Estrada, must also understand respect, a concept provided him by one Louis Hernandez. As a teen-ager, Estrada attended Menaul School in Albuquerque. He played guard for the Menaul football team and Louis Hernandez was the coach. In 1937, Estrada's last year at Menaul, the team, frequently contesting much larger schools with much bigger players, went unbeaten, untied, and unscored upon. "Mr. Hernandez taught me how to get along with people. To him that meant only one thing: respecting them. If children see a teacher respects them, they respect that teacher. As a teacher, in a little community like this, you have to set an example."

There seems to be a direct correlation between Estrada's future here and the future of the Conchas Dam Elementary School. Indeed, when the village of Trementina asked Estrada to come back, Conchas Dam rallied and fought hard to retain him, as if his presence might keep the tiny schoolhouse alive. But there is another side to this story. Explains a woman in the Conchas Dam Post Office: "We love our Mr. Estrada."

You ask people just *why* Estrada is loved and they respond, like the woman in the post office, that it is because he gives the kids individual attention, that he gets them reading instead of watching television, that he hugs them. Still, you sense there is something more. In a while the answer comes, and of course it has much to do with setting an example.

In 1978, Onofre Estrada, Rey's wife, died after losing a short fight to cancer. The couple had been married thirty-seven years. "She made the best fresh tortillas," says her husband, his voice quaking. Then theirs was a good union? No, says a Conchas native; it was a great one. Two persons were never more in love.

Due a good pension and owning a herd of cattle, it would have been easy for Rey Estrada to retire two years ago. He didn't, though he gave it much thought. "When my wife died, I wanted to give up. I never wanted to do anything else." Because the couple's two children were married and living far away, Estrada's grief was excruciatingly hard for him to bear. The nights alone were long, as they are still; most people in this remote part of San Miguel County don't have a telephone, Estrada included. Days, he must travel twenty-seven miles each way to school in his mustard-colored pickup. That left him with a lot of time to think, to get depressed.

"I stayed with teaching," Estrada says while muching on a noonday bologna sandwich he made and eats at most meals now, "because of the little ones. They kept my spirits up. The kids are why I'm still here."

Conchas Dam Elementary School still exists, and still has one teacher, but it is not Rey Estrada. According to the West Las Vegas School District, Estrada has retired to his ranch.

Cowboys and Religion

MAGDALENA—They come from Datil and Dusty and Cliff and Chloride and some even hail from near Nutt, New Mexico. Although most have post office boxes for addresses, all know that where the mailman doesn't venture, God surely does. For these cowboys—even the ones who toil in the shadow of the Diablo Mountains in this southwestern part of the state—are gathered to express thanks to the Big Foreman Upstairs.

To these men, who talk of high feed prices and grazing land, and the BLM, this is no ordinary religious roundup. They're here to hear some doggone good preaching; to share the song of life with fellow cattlemen, some of whom haven't seen each other since a similar gathering a year ago. These annual get-togethers are called Cowboy Camp Meetings. They have been a traditional part of New Mexico since the late Ralph Hall, an itinerant preacher, got a group of cowpunchers out to the Nogal Mesa to hear the gospel in 1940. The Montosa Camp Meeting, located fourteen miles west of Magdalena, followed in 1941 and, for five days each summer since has been as regular as a sunset.

The meetings took root in a time when great distances and poor transportation hindered ranchers from getting to a church. Ralph Hall and other cowboy ministers brought the Word to the ranchers—first from a horse, then later under a tent. For many cowboys still, a camp meeting is the only chance all year to cleanse the soul. Montosa's forty acres sit undisturbed till just prior to a meeting. Then the tabernacle, or chapel, the chuckwagon, and the barbecue houses get spruced up for the Wednesday to Sunday affair.

Bob Hext was a New Mexico rancher for fifty years. Most of his fence-mending was done west of Quemado, near the Arizona border. "It was a one-suspender outfit," Hext says. "You reached my place then you had to turn around and head back. Forty miles from the nearest town." Hext says he's at this camp meeting because he's got no other place to go. If truth be known he's come to Montosa to enjoy old friends, especially Alvin Simpson, a friend since 1917. "Old Bob here," says Simpson between chaws, "he's here 'cause he knows he's going to go to hell. He just wants to find out when."

"If you think I can lie to keep up with you guys, you're wrong," says an eavesdropping Graves Evans, seventy-two. At one time Evans had 2,500 head of cattle west of Truth or Consequences; now he's retired. Other cowboys, like Gilbert Baca, are just starting out—at a career and at camp meetings. "I used to work for Mr. Simpson when I was a boy," says Baca. "Now I got my own ranch near Quemado. This new generation of cowboys, it's a different breed, I guess. We work small pastures, the horses are gentler. Heck, I've seen guys in their seventies ride horses I couldn't ride." When Baca attends New Mexico State University in the winter months, he leaves his ranch in his brother's hands. You can't learn in the classroom," says Baca. "I came here to meet some of these old-timers. You can really learn from them."

A bell signals the start of the morning worship service and Baca gets up. "I go to all five churches in Quemado," he adds. "Whichever one the cowboys go to."

Tabernacle is a family event. Husbands and wives in front, teen-agers and younger children in back. Empty seats are for Stetsons. *Bringing in the Sheaves,* and *Blessed Assurance* kick off the service. The Reverend James Aiken then delivers a sermon based on John 15:11 ("Your cup overflows.") After the service Aiken, a retired Presbyterian minister, takes time out to talk. "Used to be a whole lot more of these camps. I remember my Daddy taking me to one at Ft. Davis, Texas, sixty years ago. There are churches now, but the camps keep on, thank God. These people, they have an ingrown sense of morals. You don't find people who live cleaner. A cowboy's religion is powerful—and deep, too. The rancher's got a simple approach to faith, like Jesus Christ. And it's a faith they stand on. These men, they got a private pipeline to the Lord most of us can't touch."

Lunch follows worship. If you have to ask what's on the menu (beef) you've never been near a bunkhouse. Standing in the chow line, Andrew Gordon, now living in Albuquerque, remarks that he used to have a place on the other side of Reserve, New Mexico. What town was it in, he's asked? "Wasn't in a town," comes the obvious answer. "I'm here to see some old pals," says Gordon, his face seamed as a worn saddlebag. "Trouble is, most of my old pals are gone." Gordon is asked if he's a religious man. "Listen," he explains. "Without faith the world would run amok in a hurry, wouldn't it?"

Lunch done, it's time for some *real* conversation. For

the women, that means the business of family-raising. For the men, the business of cattle-raising. Under a cauliflower-colored sky, words come slowly to the men, but they come with a quiet certainty. After being in the oil business in South America for nine years, Bill Shivers decided to enter ranching a year and a half ago. He is now helped on his place, located between Socorro and T or C, by his father-in-law, George Copeland. Copeland helps his son-in-law because Bill Shivers couldn't make it without him. The cattle business is an uphill fight, even if Americans did eat twenty-seven billion pounds of beef last year.

"The main problem for me is the environmentalists," says Shivers. "They're putting more and more controls on us. They say this land belongs to the people and, as a result, grazing fees have skyrocketed. You have to discard the value of trying to get rich in this business."

Bill Shivers likes ranching, but he must hustle. He needs a honeybee operation and a teaching job (petroleum engineering at New Mexico Tech) to make ends meet. "Ranching does have its rewards," Shivers says. "I don't have to sit back of a desk anymore. There's pressure in ranching, but it's a different kind. Here you get back to the salt of the earth, you work with God's nature."

J. R. Walter, with 125 head of cattle down in Animas, New Mexico, speaks of God with similar reverence. "We got a little old Presbyterian church in Animas, but I'm not too 'churchy.' If you're in the ranching profession though, every day you find out there is a God. We're isolated down in Animas. You feel alone out there and you need something."

Graves Evans sees God as a Special Person in ranching. "All the old cowboys I ever knew had some belief in a Supreme Being. It's built-in. If you're an honest man and approach a man honestly, your returns are pretty good."

"But you got to watch you don't get religious indigestion," jokes Bob Hext. Pausing, Hext changes the subject. "Cowpunchin's different. Used to be when I'd come to Magdalena in a wagon it was easier for my wife to buy a year's worth of groceries than it is for her to buy one day's worth now." Hext used to move his cattle to Magdalena down Highway 60, a paved road now, but once a "driveway." At seventy-seven years of age, Hext has a half-moon shaped chunk of flesh missing from the top of his left ear. "I'm a triplet," he explains. "The ear was how they told us apart." Actually, it's skin cancer— from years under a scorching New Mexico sun—that ravaged Hext's ear. "Now they found some cancer in my pancreas," he says, matter-of-factly. "That's your sweetbread; they can't operate on it. They give me chemotherapy in Albuquerque, but that's like taking one giant dose of castor oil each morning."

Ambling off, Hext heads for the afternoon worship service. Turning for a moment he says, "The Good Lord willing, I'll see the sun come up a few more times."

Lovers

MELROSE—Back in 1908, back before William Howard Taft was elected president, back before New Mexico was a state, back even before the creators of so-called open marriage were born, O. J. Awtrey and Fannie Bell, two kids of the frontier prairie, tied a knot that has grown tighter ever since. It's sort of a square knot, sure, but no noose. And even with all the offspring it has produced, no granny knot, either.

"He was kind of cute," Fannie was saying the other day in the Awtreys' green brick Melrose home, twenty-six miles west of Clovis and a light year away from any marital clinic. "She kind of snirled up her nose when she passed by," says O. J. (the *O* is for Olen; the *J* "for whatever you want.")

Theirs has been a marriage built on swapping—of quips. "What would you do if you married a rich man?" asks O. J. of his wife. "Nothing," says Fannie. "You are a good dancer except for two things," says Fannie to her husband. "What two things?" asks O. J. Fannie: "Your feet."

They met two years before their marriage at a place called Blacktower, now the site of Clovis's Cannon Air Force

Base. Children of neighboring ranchers, O. J. Awtrey was out digging post holes for his father when fourteen-year-old Fannie Bell rode by on horseback and did that famous nose twitch. "Then one day I noticed her in a buggy with my sister," O. J. says, running a hand through a copse of white hair whose thickness has defied time. "I got to taking her home. I guess she invited me to dinner. Her father was a nice fella, but he told Fannie not to bring me home anymore."

"He kids a lot," says Fannie with a light laugh that has obviously come along often in eighty-six years. A short, dark-haired woman, she appears, as her husband, much younger than she is. "We courted for two years and were sitting on a couch when he asked me to marry him. I made up my mind right quick." Here's O. J.'s recollection: "She was afraid nobody else would ask her."

In March of 1908, the pair eloped to Decatur, Texas, riding all night by train. Arriving at 7:00 A.M. in a strange town, they went to the county clerk's office and then to a local preacher. "I was real scared," says Fannie, who had just turned sixteen. "I wrote my family a letter afterward. I know my father was hurt because I was so young." O. J. has another memory: "Somebody said later that they heard old man Bell was a-hunting me with a six-shooter."

Settling on a rented farm in Avondale, Texas, the Awtreys spent their wedding night on the floor of an unfurnished farmhouse. The years following were spent picking cotton and corn together on the spread north of Ft. Worth. Those were good and bad times, as were six more years at a farm east of Marlo, Oklahoma. On Christmas Day, 1919, the Awtreys came to New Mexico and bought eighty acres near Melrose. The town then had 1,000 people. Today there are 800.

That first year in Melrose was particularly trying. To

help keep the farm running, O. J. was forced to work in a Texas oil field. "He was gone about a week at a time, the longest we have ever been away from one another," says Fannie. "She really managed the money well," recalls O. J. "She spent what I sent her on dresses. No, really, when I came back she had bought grain for the stock and had money in the bank. I don't reckon she threw one nickel away."

By now the Awtreys had two young daughters, their only children. Later, came two grandchildren, seven great-grandchildren, and five great-greats. Yep, they know all their names. In 1939, O. J. bought into a successful farm implement business. He sold out in 1954. Ten years ago, at eighty, he retired from farming. "I quit because I was getting too lazy."

He built their Melrose home himself, including a passenger elevator to the basement where a massive upright piano, purchased early in their marriage, collects dust. "Both Fannie and me are stiff in the fingers," says O. J. He holds up an arthritically-crippled hand. Their health has otherwise been good, and they say that fact probably has much to do with giving them seventy years of marriage. "Fannie had a heart attack back in sixty-nine, and I almost lost her; she's got a pacemaker now. Me? I'm about blind and had all sorts of operations, but we're doing fine, really. Every night we say a little prayer in bed, thanking the Lord, and then we try to go to sleep. With this arthritis, some nights it takes a little longer. Generally, I feel fit as a fiddle." Fannie: "Then how come you look like a saxophone?"

"I'm thankful he's still got his right mind," says Fannie. "He still gives me a dozen red roses on my birthday." Feigning outrage, O. J. asks, "You know what a dozen red roses cost today? I could take it when they cost fifteen dollars. But twenty?"

The times as well as the price of red roses have changed, and the Awtreys readily acknowledge it. But being from a different age doesn't stop them from delivering a word or two on the art of conjugal compatability.

- On arguments. Fannie: "The best way to end a scrap is for me to put my arms around his neck and give him a big kiss. Or two." O. J.: "I can't get mad at her for too long. I don't know what I'd do without those biscuits she cooks in the morning."
- On household duties. O. J.: "Ever since we've been married, I set the table and take the dishes away. That's a lot of dishes, I know." Fannie: "I take out the garbage."
- On gifts. Fannie: "The nicest thing he ever gave me was a new Pontiac car in 1948." O. J.: "Nicest thing she ever gave me was a hit on the nose. No, really, hearing 'I love you' every day is a pretty good gift."
- On divorce. O. J.: "You'll see some people married ten, fifteen years, then separate. If you can get along that long, why not more?" Fannie: "In our time, you never heard of anyone divorcing. If you love one another, you get along somehow."
- On long marriages. Fannie: "Both of us being interested in all our two daughters were doing helped. And both of us having a respect for God." O. J.: "Our marriage wasn't luck, but we've been lucky living together. I heard of a fella up in Nevada who's been married eighty-four times in eighty-four years, all to the same girl. Then I heard about another fella who's been married thirty-six times in thirty-six years. All to different girls. Can't quite figure out either fella."

Hanging above the Awtreys' double bed is a framed "Rites of Matrimony" certificate. There it is, seventy years later, signed by the county clerk in Decatur, and one J. B.

Tidwell, "minister of the gospel." "When we get mad at each other," says Fannie, "we just look up at that." O. J. takes his wife's hand. "Will you love me when I'm old and gray?" he asks. "Come back and see us again in another seventy years," urges Fannie. "You should be able to tell then whether this marriage is working out."

By all accounts, the Awtrey marriage does seem to still be working. How do I know? Not long ago I received an invitation to their seventy-third wedding anniversary party.

Healer

MOUNTAINAIR—Taped to one corner of the large front window of 114 Broadway here is the basketball schedule for the Mountainair High School Mustangs. Stuck to another corner is a flyer advertising an upcoming FHA enchilada dinner. Resting against the bottom ledge of the window, nearly out of sight, is a tiny nameplate, the only sign marking the nature of the building. *Robert J. Saul, M.D.*, the sign says plainly.

Modesty bordering on near withdrawal has always been one of Robert Saul's strong points. But in a town with 1,000 people, nobody needs a brassy physician. What is needed is a special sort of person, one like Robert Saul. "Doctor?" said someone on Broadway the other day, someone who like just about everyone around Mountainair says the abbreviated "Doctor" rather than "Dr. Saul" and is immediately understood. "Doctor? He's one of a kind."

Country doctor is a term fighting extinction. One recent survey showed that more than 130 counties in the United States were without doctors. Central New Mexico's Torrance County, with approximately 6,000 residents, is fortunate to have two doctors. That's still not enough to handle the caseload. One doctor in Estancia has been in practice there a short time. Some think Robert Saul has been around forever.

Robert Saul is conducting a well-child clinic on the second floor of Mountainair's City Hall. A pink-cheeked man with thinning blond hair and a well-fed look, Saul is wearing a scruffy, dark-checked sports coat, a limp necktie, and blue slacks. He has the rumpled appearance of someone who means to dress well but cannot find the time or money. Lying before him is a three-year-old boy named Miguel. Saul listens to the boy's chest with a stethoscope. "You're getting to be pretty big, aren't you?" the doctor asks. Miguel, with eyes the size of oysters, smiles. The smile is a kind of payoff for Robert Saul. The doctor's eyes light up like street lamps.

"Just when you think you know everything about this kind of work, you learn something more," Saul says, putting down the stethoscope. "I know most of these children. No, I don't deliver anymore. Everybody goes to the hospital now. I haven't done a delivery in twenty years or so."

It was the war that brought him to Mountainair, Saul says. He'd been stationed at the old Bruns Army Hospital in Santa Fe. While there, he got to know an older patient, also a physician. Dr. Sidney Side, from Indiana, was a recovering POW. After leaving Bruns, Side decided to stay in New Mexico; he went to the tiny community of Mountainair. Saul returned to his hometown of Reading, Pennsylvania, to a job with the Veterans Administration. Meanwhile, Side wrote to Saul and urged him to return to New Mexico for a visit. In 1949, Saul did come. He arrived in Mountainair in November, stopped at a hotel on Broadway, and checked in. He was just looking around, he told the clerk. He was given the key to Room Eighteen. Ten thousand nights have passed and Robert Saul is still in Room Eighteen.

"What happened," Saul says, trying to understand it himself, "was that I joined Dr. Side in practice, right next to the hotel." A year later Side died. Saul inherited the practice and became only the fourth doctor in Mountainair since the town was founded in 1903.

Saul has no nurse in his office, which is located a half dozen steps from the front door of the Thomas Inn, the hotel where he lives. He has no set office hours, either. "I start in the morning and finish when I'm done. People know where I am. If they see my car out front they come in." And they do. On any given day, Saul's large waiting room is crowded like a bus station. No one makes appointments; the doctor takes people as they enter the door—an old man with ulcers, a young housewife with a backache, a little boy with worms. "I don't like to keep patients waiting three hours like some of those doctors in Albuquerque do," says Saul. A middle-aged Hispanic woman was in the other day, he says, a mother who complained of exhaustion. She had twenty-two children at home. Saul saw her immediately.

Saul's examining room adjoins his private office. His desk, despite his secretary's good intentions, is a forest of knickknacks, unpaid bills, letters, prescriptions, food wrappers. A visitor notices an ornamental globe sticking out from under a pile of papers. "That's a present," Saul says. "So's that," he adds, pointing to a barometer on the wall. "And that," to an oil painting. Dozens of gadgets, many expensive, litter the room. All gifts. "It gets me so darn mad when people give me these things. I wish they wouldn't do it." Saul's tone is unmistakable: he's proud. After all, what doctor in the country charges seven dollars and twenty-eight cents for an office visit? It's pretty well known around Mountainair that if you're in a financial pinch, you can toss Doctor's bill to the dust and let the rain settle it. Saul himself laughs about unpaid bills. In fact he knows a joke about them. A doctor told a man he had six months to live. "Six months?" the man said. "I don't think I can pay my bill." "Okay," says the doctor. "Then I'll give you another six months."

Saul may be slightly disorganized but one must not mistake that for inability. "He's one smart doctor," says Mike Kelley, who runs the pharmacy in Mountainair. "A person might expect that a little town like ours would have a not very sharp doctor. It's just the opposite. Where most doctors know about one drug to use in a particular case, Doctor might know six." Saul's thirst for medical knowledge came from one C. J. Dietrich, his own family doctor back in Pennsylvania. Dietrich was a stern-looking man, forbidding at times. "But I knew if I went to him," Saul recalls, "I'd get well. He was good and kind. He was the type of man I wanted to be." From his schoolteacher mother Saul came to experience the pleasures of reading and a desire for education. This led to study at Gettysburg College and then at Jefferson Medical College in Philadelphia, from which he was graduated in 1943. Saul learned something else from his mother. "She told me if I was going to go into medicine for the money, I was crazy."

There is one more baby in the clinic for Saul to see before it is time for lunch. It is a small boy with bruises on his legs. "He was in a car crash not long ago and broke his leg," Saul explains. Auto wrecks and farm accidents are a big part of Saul's work. Car crashes—along Highway 14, the road that winds through little mountain towns like

Torreon and Tajique—are frequent. When Saul's telephone rang one weekend afternoon last year, it signaled one of the most tragic events ever in Mountainair. A couple had been out on Highway 14 when their eight-year-old daughter, sitting on the back of the pickup, suddenly fell off and under the wheels of a car in back. The girl was rushed to Presbyterian Hospital in Albuquerque and Saul went with the family. The child died, and as with almost anything that happens to the people of Mountainair, her death touched Saul deeply. "When you're sick," says one resident, "Doctor's sick. When you cry, he cries."

Lunchtime for Saul means the Golden Grill Cafe. Located directly across from his office and hotel room, it is the Golden Grill where Saul takes nearly all his meals. The moment he sits down in the tidy, well-lighted restaurant, waitresses begin fussing over him. "You know," says one, "when Doctor came out here from Pennsylvania he wasn't too crazy about Spanish food. But he is now, and we're crazy about him. What other person could come in here and order half an egg on an enchilada and get away with it?" Lois Granger, owner of the Golden Grill, says she is closed on Saturday nights. "But if I find Doctor doesn't have any place to go, I'll come down here special and open up and fix him something. That's why he's always saying his family is here in Mountainair. He's adopted us and we have him."

On Saul's twenty-fifth year of practice in Mountainair, residents bought him a new car. The car—a beige Chevrolet—is like a landmark on Broadway. When it's parked in front of his office, all seems well. The car is seldom *not* there. He is a bachelor who takes few vacations. "I've been interested in marriage," he says with a shy smile. "But nothing ever really progressed. Anyway, I don't know how a man would get along with a wife in a job like this. I think if you're in this business, you owe it to the people to be here."

On his way out of the Golden Grill Saul is approached by Abran Garcia, Mountainair's chief of police. The two are close; last year a crazed former patient of Saul's charged into the physician's office waving a rifle and looking for drugs. "Doctor," says Garcia, "he kept his cool. When the man gave him an order, Doctor just told him to go away. Even after the man fired a couple of shots, Doctor just walked out the front door. Doctor? He's just a real fine man. I don't know what we'd do if he wasn't around."

Rarely do I hear from anyone I write about; not that I expect to, of course. In fact, I often fear it. Robert Saul, who continues to practice in Mountainair, did send me a nice note after this story appeared. "It's going to very hard in the future of my life," he wrote, "to live up to the high standards that were alluded to me in your article."

Washed Away

ALBUQUERQUE—Novelist Thomas Wolfe may have decreed that one can't return to one's original domicile, but don't tell that to housewife Edith Black. She says even if your home isn't there anymore it's still a pleasure to go back. Edith Black? "People may not know me," says the seventy-four-year-old Mrs. Black, sounding much like a credit card commercial. "But they sure should know where I'm from—San Marcial, New Mexico. That's the town was wiped out by the flood."

The year was 1929, just prior to the fall of Wall Street. The Russians were skirmishing the Chinese in Manchuria. The Philadelphia Athletics were pummelling the Yankees in the American League. Thirty miles south of Socorro, New Mexico, it was business as usual in the community of San Marcial (pronounced *Mar-shell*). Gray Hanna was adding new shelves to his grocery. Postmaster Epigmenio Ramirez wondered when a stamp would go from two cents to three. Over at the Harvey House, the busy restaurant and hotel, the talk was all Herbert Hoover. In the railway yard, machinist Lencho Barela, clerk Les Parker, and fireman Jack Tabor were doing what San Marcial was known for: railroading. A division point on the Santa Fe, San Marcial was one of the great rail centers of the Southwest. One who labored there was called with respect a "Horny Toad Man," after the pesky creatures that patrolled the tracks between Albuquerque and El Paso.

Floods gave San Marcial additional fame. Founded in the seventeenth century by priests of the conquistadores, San Marcial had always known water. Supposedly the town was originally built on an ancient Indian pueblo. Some said the Indians had vanished when the unpredictable river sent them packing once too often. Straddling a turbulent spot beneath the west bank of the Rio Grande, San Marcial sat just below the tributary points of the Rio Puerco and Rio Salado. Records show that the town was hit by major floods in 1886, 1900, and 1912. "Heck," says Edith Black, "high water in town was pretty much a yearly thing." Records also show that each time a flood struck, San Marcial rebuilt. Then came 1929. On August thirteenth, a wall of moving water turned the community upside down. In two days the city of 2,000 was buried under ten feet of silt. Miraculously, San Marcial dug out and resurrected itself. A month later, on September twenty-third, a second, more devastating flood brought the place to its knees.

Like its most famous resident—the steam locomotive—San Marcial ceased to exist. And yet to the many who lived there before that second flood, San Marcial endures. Nearly every year since the city's demise, reunion picnics have been held in New Mexico, or in Long Beach, California, where many Santa Fe Railway employees have retired. Recently, thirty-three former San Marcial residents gathered at an Albuquerque park to travel back in time to a town that Edith Black says was "one of the nicest places on earth." For the outsider, only through a picnic can San

Marcial be visualized. Save for some weed-dressed stone foundations and a jungle of cottonwood trees, there is nothing in San Marcial, not even a trace of the roundhouse that covered two city blocks. "It's a ghost town," says Esther May Comstock, born there eighty-four years ago. "San Marcial's plumb gone except for here," she says, tapping her chest.

Fay Webster arrived in San Marcial when he was eight. Like his father before him, Webster joined the railroad when he was a teen-ager. He stayed with it forty-seven years. "San Marcial sure was a sociable place," Webster recalls. "If anybody had any problems we all pitched in, especially if the river was raising cain which it was known to do." In those days when the Corps of Engineers was a stranger to the region, living several feet below the Rio Grande was dangerous. A little rain here and there and you had a backwater flood in San Marcial. If you were a Horny Toad Man, you knew all there was to know about shoring up dikes and levees.

After half a century of railroading, John Mackey settled in Los Angeles ten years ago. A machinist's apprentice in San Marcial in 1919, Mackey remembers a flood *that* year. "The water came up to within four inches of my mattress, but I stayed in bed. You got used to it." Esther May Comstock, daughter of a locomotive engineer, can remember a 1910 flood. "My mother looked up and saw water coming in the ceiling. Next thing I know she emptied a bureau draw into a pillow case and was on her way out the door with me." Helen Parker, daughter of a San Marcial banker, recalls swimming in the Rio Grande as a girl. "You had to be careful about diving, though. The river depth changed so much from day to day."

Jack Tabor and his wife, Mary, honeymooned in San Marcial just before the final flood. "A young couple could feel right at home in the town," says Tabor. "Small enough for you to know everybody; big enough so's you had to keep your mouth shut. Know what I mean?" There were moonlight strolls to the iron bridge, ukelele serenades, and flappers to gawk at. "Tame by today's standards," says Mary Tabor with a giggle. "Lots of fun then."

Charles Hayes, a former three-star general in the Marine Corps, has called many spots home: Hawaii, San Diego, Newport, Rhode Island, the South Pacific, Florida. "As great places to live," says Hayes, "I'd have to rate San Marcial high up on that list." Hayes was a midshipman at the Naval Academy when the September 1929 flood arrived. "My parents wired me; I was real sorry."

Herman Roser was only seven in 1929 but the significance San Marcial played in his early life is sharply etched. "The fact that I was born and lived there," says Roser, manager of the U.S. Department of Energy's Albuquerque office, "made me more self-reliant, I think. It was a great place for a kid to grow up, and I mean grow." Clear in Roser's memory are peeks he took into the ornate San Marcial Opera House, glimpses he got of the traveling Chautauqua shows, and the hero-worshipping he did over San Marcial's fine baseball team (Fay Webster played left field, Lencho Barela pitched.) Though violence was nearly unknown in San Marcial, Roser remembers seeing a man shot to death on Main Street during a drunken brawl. As so many others were, Roser was put on a train to El Paso minutes before the September flood. A couple of months later, the Roser family returned to San Marcial to survey the damage. Because the outpouring came with almost no warning, nearly everyone lost nearly everything. Roser's father lost a prized library, and the family's piano perished. A crocheted bed spread was recovered. Roser's wife has it now and it is treasured highly. Roser lost a special pedal-operated car. "I went digging for it," he says, "and when I found it it was all rusted and useless." Herman Roser says holding that broken toy was one of the few moments in his life when he has cried openly.

Depending upon one's status with the railroad, one either lived on "Society Row" (for Santa Fe brass), or "Ice House Row" (for brakemen and laborers, mostly). There was money in San Marcial—B. A. West, the railroad supervisor, was well-off. But most people, like Charles White, were not. Now living in Newhall, California, White came to San Marcial in 1920 to begin work as an apprentice telegrapher. A bachelor, he earned sixty dollars a month. Was the single life good there? a fellow picnicker asks White. "I was so damn tired," he answers, "and so damn broke, I could never do much entertaining." Though Main Street wasn't Broadway, it was lively, even if few cars prowled its dirt stretches. Anyway, if you really wanted to go someplace, you took the train. Meeting spots along Main were the Harvey House, of course, and even during Prohibition, the Wigwam Saloon. The Wigwam was owned by Ishmael Ortega. His son, Lelo, lives in Albuquerque. A widower early, Lelo raised six children in San Marcial, none of whom he says with sadness cares much for the town's legacy. Lelo stayed on in San Marcial after the last disaster. He lived with his children in a house on high ground. He worked odd jobs, but there wasn't much going. When Eppie Ramirez closed the post office in the mid-1930s, the town pretty much called it quits. Today, San Marcial isn't even on some state maps.

Geographically, San Marcial was actually three communities: New Town, which was mostly Anglo; Old Town, which was entirely Hispanic; in between was known as Midway. "Didn't matter what part of town you were from," points out Rosie Barela, who is Lencho's wife and Lelo's sister. "It was all one family. You cared about everyone." This was especially true on that Monday morning in September when a two-story-high wall of river water roared through town and washed away everything. In the face of personal peril, race mattered not a whit. If you were a San Marcialite, and you saw another in trouble, you gave a hand. Charlie Nattress led those who couldn't swim onto a railroad tie and floated with them to the top of the Harvey House, one of the few dry spots. Gray Hanna rowed down Main Street searching for stranded refugees. Before water blasted through the downstairs of the railroad depot, O. E. Roser, Herman's father, cut the telegraph wires, carried them upstairs, and summoned Socorro and other places for help.

Too much was wiped out in that flood to think of rebuilding. Despite the terrible destruction, no one was killed. In fact, no one was injured. That in a sense may help explain why San Marcialites feel their community was so rare. Esther Comstock puts it this way: "San Marcial was a place God loved." All that God has left behind are yellowed snapshots and picnics. While it is good to get together annually, picnickers say what hurts is that each year the reunions are attended by fewer and fewer former residents. Never mind, though: so long as any San Marcialite is alive, grit and determination persists. It's all around. Fay Webster had a recent prostate operation, but he's back bowling again; Herman Roser just underwent open heart surgery, but he's returned to his desk at the Department of Energy; and Gray Hanna, near ninety and quite frail, still has a quick and nimble mind.

Following this year's picnic, Edith Black and John Mackey, Californians now, planned to return to their adopted homestate—but not before making a sidetrip to San Marcial. "After all," says Mackey, "it's just off the highway."

Except for a cemetery (where some Hannas, Blacks and Ortegas lie side by side) there would seem little reason to leave that highway. "You don't understand," explains Edith Black. "I just want to look around and remember. You see, there just won't ever be another town quite like San Marcial."

Good news and bad. First the bad: Gray Hanna has died at age ninety-one. Now the good: The San Marcial Reunion Committee recently released this notice: "Picnics will continue to be held come rain or shine."

3: Achievers

"It wouldn't bother me if my ladies appeared on paper cups."

The Selling of an Artist

TAOS—An apricot-colored telephone is ringing in R. C. Gorman's sitting room. The artist reaches for it instinctively, giving some support to the growing belief that these days Gorman uses a phone more than a paint brush. On the other end of the telephone is a woman—a stranger with a strange request. She wishes to use Gorman's Jacuzzi for a private "rebirthing" ceremony: she'd like to climb into Gorman's water and "climb back" into the womb.

The forty-eight-year-old Gorman is tickled by the woman's request; on the other hand he is bugged. He turns her down politely. "I can't have odd creatures using my home for such things," he tells a visitor. "Do you have any idea what it costs me just to turn on my Jacuzzi? If someone wants to come over and mop my swimming pool, fine. But a . . . what did she call it? . . . a rebirth? Gorman laughs. A deep tummy laugh it is. *Har-dee-har-har.*

It makes sense that the more R. C. Gorman heads toward incorporating, a direction in which many believe he's moving, the more he needs a telephone. Besides the offbeat proposals from assorted sycophants, many calls to

Gorman's three million dollar adobe home do have to do with business: his lawyers, Leo Kelly or Tim Sheehan of Albuquerque, Hank Messinger of Taos; his Taos gallery director, Virginia Dooley; his secretary, Rosalie Talbott; his Albuquerque gallery director, Scott Poland; his painting assistant, Curtis Grubbs; his ceramicist, Greg Grycner; the firms that do his lithographs; the many galleries that show them. Asks one cynic: "Why does Gorman need all those people? Why can't he just paint?"

To his credit, or perhaps athwart it, Gorman does not employ an agent. This may surprise those who are convinced he is being manipulated by some gone-wild promoter. "I find it safer when I'm in charge," Gorman says, gulping a second noontime rum drink his housekeeper, Rose Roybal, has set before him. "A lot of people from New York call and say they want to handle my business affairs, advise me. They say I'm out of control. Look, I don't need people to tell me when I can use my bidet."

Virginia Dooley is probably the closest thing he has to a Svengali. Yet she has tried and failed to talk Gorman out of various commercial deals, including his recent contract with Goldwaters for which Gorman drew severe criticism. "Gorman couldn't benefit from an agent," Ms. Dooley explains. "I don't think anyone would understand him as a Navajo. He has to be allowed to be as free as possible. He tries to watch the quality of the stuff he's associated with, but it's not always possible. His decisions always prove right, though. He knows what he's doing." "Gorman has the final word," says Scott Poland. "Nobody is using him."

If R. C. Gorman is not being used, he is being dissected, like a giant pie. The result is many pieces, some with frosting, some just plain dough. For those who believe they can't turn around without bumping into something by R. C. Gorman, and wonder how he can do it all, the answer is he doesn't. When you are a multi-million dollar empire, you must have help. Haag and Haag Diversified Art in Tucson is an "artistic" wholesaler that works with 150 stores, mostly in the Southwest. Haag's clients run from Goldwaters to tiny boutiques. Haag sells Gorman poster prints in several large sizes. Prices range from fifty dollars to $150, unsigned. Haag also peddles three sizes of Gorman lithograph reproductions. These retail for sixteen dollars to twenty dollars, unsigned.

The company markets a three-inch-tall Gorman-styled Indian woman figurine. The statue comes in pewter, copper, or brass and retails for fifty-five dollars. Haag also fashions eleven variations of Gorman pottery, with an average price of fifty dollars per object. The pots feature an imprint of a Gorman woman. The words *R. C. Gorman* are stamped on. Decorative tiles are another Haag novelty. They come in half a dozen sizes and sell for around forty-five dollars.

Jerry Haag, like most who handle Gorman reproductions, will not reveal what—if any—artistic contributions Gorman provides. Nor does Haag offer apologies for what the company is doing. "Our creations make Gorman's artwork available to the great majority who can't afford the real thing," says Haag. "It in no way cheapens his work."

Sandstone Creations, in Tempe, Arizona, first published a Gorman greeting card nine years ago. The wholesale outfit has since joined forces with the artist in many areas, all designed to bring Gorman into Sandstone's 2,500 retail outlets. A hot Sandstone item is a R. C. Gorman wind chime that goes for eighteen dollars. Sandstone turns these out in three models, and says they are selling at the rate of 750 a month. Gorman's Sandstone note paper comes in seven patterns. The paper sells for three dollars a box. More than 10,000 boxes are sold each month. Other Sandstone sundries doing well are the R. C. Gorman Christmas cards which come in eight styles, and individual Gorman cards. "Other than DeGrazia (the assembly-line artist from Arizona), Gorman is our biggest seller," says Sandstone's Mike Chiricuzio. "We're talking to him now about a large wall calendar, a dinner bell, and three more wind chime designs."

SAGA Inc. (Southwestern Artists and Graphics) is based in Albuquerque. It wholesales to 1,000 markets and channels the following Gorman goods: nine styles of note paper, two brands of stationary, individual cards, and Christmas cards. "We find people either really like Gorman or really hate him," says Joanne Brookover who, with her husband, Bill, runs SAGA. "We sell as much as we can print."

Although R. C. Gorman is not a writer, books featuring his work do extremely well. Gorman's book publisher is Northland Press, of Flagstaff, Arizona. In August 1978, Northland came out with *The Lithographs,* a coffee-table tome costing thirty-seven fifty. The book, which has yet to go into paperback, is now in its third printing. Another Gorman book, *The Posters,* is available in both paper and hardbound, for fourteen-ninety-five, and twenty-five dollars respectively. Total sales for both books is 15,000. "That may not sound like a lot," says Chris Knoell, Northland's sales manager, "but for an artist it's quite good, expecially when you consider the price." Knoell says Gorman is Northland's best-selling author. "The commercialism you keep hearing about hasn't hurt his book sales. After all, you see Old Masters on greeting cards."

The crown jewel for most of these companies was captured when all Goldwaters department stores opened what is essentially a "Gorman Room." If Goldwaters had any second thoughts about vending a fine artist alongside bath mats, those thoughts have since disappeared. Says one salesperson in the Albuquerque store: "Gorman's doing better than anything on the floor. He's topped our Nambé shop. We can't keep him in stock."

The telephone in Taos is ringing again. This time it is an old friend who seeks Gorman's advice. She has been married eight times, once to writer Frank Waters. She wonders if she should take a ninth husband. "Do it," Gorman urges. "It might be fun." *Har-dee-har-har.*

Gorman has never married. His life's tale is well known: born Rudolph Carl Gorman in a hogan on the Navajo Reservation in Chinle, Arizona, he was an earnest artist with an elegant vision of the American Indian by the mid-1960s. To say his vision caught on would be an understatement. When Gorman is lolling about his $150,000 indoor swimming pool surrounded by sculpture of male genitalia, one question becomes self-revealing: Does he ever think back to the days when he didn't have an indoor toilet? This elicits no laugh. Another rum drink is summoned. Then: "I had it better in Chinle. The water there was running. It was muddy water, but it was free and healthy and beautiful. Now they've dammed up that river. They've cut down the cottonwoods and replaced them with filling stations."

There's another reason why Gorman can't go home again. One can hardly take to Chinle a wall of photographs of Lucille Ball, Mae West, and Liz Taylor, not to mention Warhol canvases and a gold Mercedes. To be sure there are signs of home in his Taos place, or at least hominess: a framed certificate of recognition from a 4-H group; a trophy belonging to the Taos women's softball team Gorman sponsors. The squad's name really is "Me and My R. C.s."

When Gorman built his new Taos manse smack on a

heavily-trafficked highway instead of some private back road, more than one person felt he stopped trying as an artist. Indeed, one has to speculate when Gorman *does* do his art. A blank drawing pad stands idle. Gorman says he can't work at home: the telephone. And he can't work in his downtown Taos gallery: the gawkers. Adjoining his house, a monstrous studio with twenty-foot ceilings is under construction. "It will be used for art," says Gorman, "or it will be an airplane hangar." *Har-dee-har-har.*

If Gorman toils at his craft, as he swears he does, his detractors are quick to point out he has an army of assistants. The artist nods—he has help, he admits. Outside interests require it. Rarely does Gorman turn down an interview, a vacation, a party. That may be part of the problem. The other part is: Has R. C. Gorman become too busy being a celebrity to ever again make a true commitment to his art? Gorman scoffs at the thought. "An artist loses his sense of responsibility when he thinks his time is too precious."

If Gorman has become an underachiever, then why does he appear to be over-exposed? An interesting way to answer this is to draw a parallel between Gorman and Fritz Scholder, another New Mexico artist, and part Indian. The novice sometimes confuses Gorman and Scholder; never the judge. Recently, certain critics ordered that Scholder should be taken seriously; that Gorman should not. Scholder hardly ever talks to the press. Gorman hams it up for any journalist in sight. While Scholder once cranked out lithographs at a Gorman-like clip, he mostly does originals now—something Gorman seldom does. And Scholder's originals outsell Gorman.

If Gorman is being artistically eclipsed by Fritz Scholder, can Ted DeGrazia be far behind? Many reviewers say yes. DeGrazia, the mass marketeer whose Indian Munchkins adorn everything from kitchen plates to hand towels, appeals, sniffs one culture-watcher, "to people in Hawaiian shirts and black knee socks."

"Yes, I hear there are people who say I'm in danger of becoming a DeGrazia," says Gorman, reaching for a drink. "I think it's mostly being said by artists who haven't been offered what I have. Cruel dealers, too. How can you consider stationary and other reproductions works of art? It wouldn't bother me if my ladies appeared on paper cups."

The wrinkle in all this is that if R. C. Gorman has become a spin-off king, dispensed in chain stores like cheap china, he is, of course, also being sold in art galleries—his original marketplace. Fine art galleries have little use for wind chimes. They handle Gorman's lithographs, his signed posters, what oils and acrylics he does: the top-drawer material. Still, galleries are part of the pie.

Gorman owns two galleries named Navajo—one in Taos, one in Albuquerque. Both feature his work almost solely. Additionally, an Enthios Gallery in Santa Fe and one in Albuquerque carry a high percentage of Gorman. Northern New Mexico does not have a lock on the artist, however. Nearly thirty galleries around the country, from Wichita, Kansas, to Weston, Massachusetts, have "representational" contracts with Gorman. That is, they display other artists but have Gorman under personal contract for lithographs and originals.

To discover how well a Gorman gallery does, one need only drop in on his Navajo Gallery in Albuquerque's Old Town. Scott Poland is the manager, and between the flood of tourists and phone orders, Poland barely has a free moment. Lithographs in Navajo go for $500 to $2,500. An original oil starts at $4,000 and can climb to $18,000. On top of this, Navajo sells limited editions of ceramics for fifty dollars to $150. Gorman bronzes go for $6,000 to

$12,000. "And of course," says Poland, "we sell a hell of a lot of posters." Poland acknowledges hearing the complaint that Gorman is spreading himself too thin, reaching in too many directions, selling out. "An artist as prolific as Gorman and as successful, it's hard for him to hold down his energy. Gorman can't flood the market because the market for Gorman is worldwide." Unabashedly, Poland admits he could sell almost anything of Gorman's especially if it bore the man's signature. As a way of explanation, Poland holds up an agreeable if undistinguished post card invitation to an upcoming Gorman show in Paris. "If I could get Gorman to sign this, and then put it in a frame, I could get fifty dollars."

At Albuquerque's Enthios Gallery, Liz Mendez says she sells an average of two Gorman lithographs and ten to twelve posters every week. Despite such prosperity, Ms. Mendez is annoyed. "Gorman's a super artist, but I think he's lowered himself. I hate to see him on napkins and all." In Santa Fe's Enthios Gallery, Marian Frank feels she is in a tough position. "I don't want to hurt the good relationship I have with Gorman. But what does a gallery owner say to a client who comes in and tells you he saw a Gorman in JC Penney? An art gallery is a very special type of place. You are not five-and-dimeing it."

Criticism of the Gorman explosion is not confined to local art salons. Marjorie Kauffman owns two galleries in Houston. Both represent Gorman and each sells from four to five of his lithographs daily. Ms. Kauffman is hesitant to speak out, but does say, "R. C. is the kind of guy who won't say no to anybody. I have bawled him out about giving his name to things like tiles, but he says, 'These people are my old friends'." Although she doesn't foresee a shortage of Gormanphiles, Ms. Kauffman is bothered by the great number of Gorman lithographs, works that at this moment are appreciating nicely. "I think he's being pressured to do more work by his publishers (the people who print his lithographs). I can sell them, but it worries me."

Troubled, too, is Christopher Bayard Condon who operates the Bayard Gallery in New York City. Not long ago the Bayard held a Gorman show that was a smash. Even so Condon says he will never again stock a Gorman lithograph. "I think his publishers are exploiting him mercilessly. I signed an exclusive with Gorman only to find his publishers were dealing the same lithographs other places. I've written them, I've written Gorman. All I get back are snide replies. This may have to go into litigation." Condon's wrath builds when the topic is Gorman's mercantilism. "In Seattle, Gorman shows at the most commercial gallery, the one that handles LeRoy Neiman (the middlebrow sports scenographer). Gorman stands to destroy his reputation as a fine artist. He's become a media event. The Gorman balloon could pop and he could be out in the cold."

All kitsch aside, Gorman's main source of income continues to be his lithographs. A lithograph is printed from a piece of stone on which an artist has drawn an impression. Three printers take care of Gorman's lithographs: Origins Press in Tubac, Arizona, Houston Fine Arts in Texas, and Western Graphics in Albuquerque. Several times each year Gorman will visit one of his publishers. He will sit down in their office and create one of his Indian women. The publisher will then give him a choice of color combinations and Gorman will choose up to three. Gorman's first "state," or series of lithographs printed, numbers 150, a fairly high figure compared with other artists. A second state provides another 150. A third state will yield fifty to seventy more. What irks some gallery owners is that the large quantity often lessens the quality.

Simple arithmetic may help explain why a Gorman publisher would push for more lithographs. At $700 each, say, 350 editions of a lithograph could mean at least $350,000 to divvy up. A publisher usually gets the even-numbered editions to wholesale to galleries. Gorman gets the odd numbers and normally sells them through his Navajo galleries or elsewhere.

In defense of the high volume of lithographs, Western Graphics's Richard Godbold states flatly, "Based on the law of supply and demand, it could be said that not enough are being done." Virginia Dooley, who tries to monitor Gorman's lithograph output, compounds the situation by revealing that Gorman can't accept any more galleries from a long list that wait to represent him. Says Ms. Dooley: "We just don't have the work."

Once more the telephone interrupts. "Yes, yes," whispers Gorman, ". . . of course I'll throw you a party . . . we'll float gardenias in the swimming pool. . . ."

Ted DeGrazia, who would never wear gardenias, became famous—and rich—by duplicating little Indians. The criticism of Gorman is that he's doing the same thing with his ladies, his Earth Women; that he just moves them into different poses and changes the colors. "That Indian woman is beautiful," says one Taos artist, "but three dozen times is enough."

Never change a winning game goes the old saw. Gorman has always been popular because he makes the American West contemporary and universal. "His lithographs are controversial," explains Marjorie Kauffman. "They're pleasant." Yet the winning game is beginning to show signs of wear. Bill Peterson edits *Artspace*, a respected journal of southwestern art. Once an admirer, Peterson has become disenchanted with Gorman. "It seems to me he has let his art go; he's repeating himself. The fact that Gorman knows Andy Warhol tells me Gorman is playing a game with his audience. I've heard rumors that Gorman doesn't even do his lithographs by himself anymore."

Chris Condon says, "The majority of people who buy Gorman lithographs are not real art collectors. Those who buy his original oils (which never feature his Indian women) know fine art. I'd much rather have an original Gorman oil. They're harder to sell, but they're genius."

Gorman has heard all this a million times. "I'm secure with my ladies. Why should I paint landscapes one day, mad dogs the next? An artist does what he can do best. I'll stop painting ladies when they stop making them." *Hardee-har-har.*

Mathematics may again be used to understand why Gorman stays away from originals. A Gorman oil, a one-shot deal, might sell for $8,000. A single lithograph can reap 10 times that. Based on this country's free enterprise system, R. C. Gorman certainly has the right to do what he pleases. When that right is challenged, it's because this same country demands the most of a person's gifts. One gallery owner puts it this way: "Gorman doesn't do many originals anymore because he's lazy." Chris Condon believes Gorman has been presented with a choice: fine art or money. Sighs Condon, "He went for the money."

For R. C. Gorman, for any artist who considers himself dedicated, the question of money will always prick the conscience. Gorman deals with any guilt feelings by donating drawings to charity, by earmarking certain profits to aid young students. At the same time, Gorman is no easy touch. He has stopped doling out loans indiscriminately. The revelries he often plays host for won't cease, however; the man likes to have fun. Trips to Antibes won't stop, nor the caviar in bed. All that is part of Gorman, the onetime altar boy. "Let's face it," says Scott Poland. "He's no hermit."

Fact is he frets about finances. "Doesn't everybody? The government takes half of what I make." Like a good entrepreneur he looks for an edge. He may run sheep on his sprawling Taos property for "tax purposes." Money should not have that much to do with signing autographs, but for Gorman it does. All his lithographs, of course, bear his signature. The Gorman posters dealers sell also carry his hand; it brings an extra twenty dollars. Gorman says he would like to stop signing the posters—"a pain in the groin"—but can't.

Curiously, he owns an autograph book. He has his housekeeper fetch it for the visitor, along with another rum for himself. Allen Ginsberg is in the book; so is Elizabeth Taylor. "You big brown man . . ." Liz scribbled affectionately.

Gorman tells of attending a party and being asked for his autograph by a young man. As Gorman reached for a pen, the fan dropped his trousers and requested Gorman sign right there—on the derriere. The artist obliged. "Do you know what that fellow did then?" Gorman asks in a voice that suggests R. C. is nobody's fool, that R. C. will *always* have the final word, the last laugh, especially on the way to the bank. "That fellow showed my autograph around for two hours. At two dollars a peek, he ended up making eighty dollars." *Har-dee-har-har.*

Few stories I've written generated as much wrath from readers as this. I still can't figure why. I like Gorman, as his signed poster print on my living room wall will attest.

Local Hero

ALBUQUERQUE—Bobby Foster has a headache. He is sitting in a South Valley luncheonette, smoking a Viceroy between sips of coffee. Neither helps the pain that penetrates the bridge of his nose. The migraines have been coming on a lot lately, says the former light heavyweight boxing champion of the world. At first Foster thought it was sinuses. When the headaches didn't go away he went to a physician. "You know what the doctor said? Told me I should stop hating people."

Bobby Foster bears a grudge? Wasn't he Mr. Nice Guy once? Once upon a time Foster was many things. He was a celebrity who had clout, an eminence with a glamorous wife, friends, money. Now he calls himself a forty-one-year-old cop with a .357 revolver, an out-of-shape memento of a man who gets booed at local prize fights and hooted in the city he loves—and sometimes, dislikes. Stories of ex-pugilists who have fallen on hard times are legion. "Hey, babe," says Foster. "It ain't all that bad." But when this former fighter takes off his tinted beige sunglasses and you check out the eyes (only a little scar tissue), a wounded spirit is unmistakable.

The most recent issue of *Ring* magazine names Foster Boxer of the Decade for all light heavyweights. It's a tribute that should make him happy. These days, however, few things make Bobby Foster very happy. Spread in front of him this morning is a newspaper photograph of an aging and flabby Muhammad Ali at work on yet another comeback. Ali was never a friend of Foster's; the picture only makes Bobby's head hurt worse. "Ten years ago you couldn't hit Ali in the ass with a thing. But now? He's crazy to fight again. I'd never do it. Who'd want to see me anyway?"

At one time a lot of people did. Bob Foster had the city of Albuquerque eating out of his big-knuckled hand. Two appreciation days were held in his honor. He was a local hero, born and bred here. Now he is more than a touch bitter. He earned two million dollars in the ring. It's gone and so is the applause. "Name something good that's happened to me in the last few years?" he repeats the question while lighting another cigarette. A hollow laugh follows; the sunglasses go back on. "Nothing."

Indeed, since he quit boxing in 1974, Foster's life has been anything but tranquil. In 1976, he was divorced from his wife of twenty years. It was a nasty split, he says. Pearl Foster and their four children now live in Pennsylvania. The break-up was only the beginning of his troubles. A series of incidents in his job as a deputy for the Bernalillo County Sheriff's Department tarnished a once unsullied image. He was accused of cheating on a departmental examination (the charges were dropped). Failure to pass a firearms test caused him to be suspended without pay (he was reinstated a few days later). In 1977, he was sued for $350,000 by a man who Foster shot during a burglary investigation (the case was settled out of court).

Two years ago, Foster wed again, this time to a white woman seventeen years his junior. The marriage didn't work. "We're still good friends, though," he says. Last year was the worst. The first divorce settlement, the child support he still pays to his youngest daughter, the pursuit of bill collectors of every sort ("Like a lot of folks, they bled me to death") caught up with him. Bob Foster filed for bankruptcy. "It was embarrassing," he admits.

Foster blames his lifestyle—and certain people. There is no denying that during the early 1970s Bob Foster lived regally. His sprawling South Valley ranch-style home had four bedrooms, two fireplaces, three baths, a swimming pool in the back, horses in an adjoining field. In the driveway was a new Mark IV every year, a Cadillac, a couple of motorcycles, a Corvette. There was always plenty of money when Foster was fighting for $200,000 purses.

Then where did it all go? Foster rubs his forehead; the pain is back. "I know one thing," he says. "I'll never let anybody look after my money. I'll never own another credit card." The lavishness, he says, spoiled everyone—especially his children. He is not close to any of them now except Tony, twenty-one. Mention of his other son makes Foster wince. Bobby Jr., twenty-three, was involved in some minor scrapes with police here.

Once the money began going, it went fast and nothing took its place. Promised movie roles didn't pan out. A book on Foster's life never got off the ground. Always an intensely prideful man, Foster remains so. "I'm the same as I always was," he insists. "It's other people who have changed." But some other people feel Foster is just too stubborn; when he was strapped and debt-ridden, he refused to ask for help.

Foster waves away this notion. He is a man, he says. He doesn't accept handouts. Still, an offer would have been nice. "Somebody once told me when you're at the top everybody cares about you. When you're not, nobody knows you. That's true. Used to be I had a whole lot of leeches 'round me. Not anymore." Foster claims Billy Edwards, his trainer for twenty years, won't return a telephone call. Edwards responds, "Bobby wants things to be the same as when he fought. Life just don't work that way."

A detective in the violent crimes division, Foster would like to be doing something else. "Who wants to bust people, make enemies? That's got to be why I get booed." What he would like to do is run a boxing club or do public relations for the sheriff's department. "Man, this chasing guys down ditchbanks wears on you. I want to work with kids. Hey, babe, juveniles are the ones who are committing all the crimes."

Again, self-respect seems to keep Foster from doing what he wants. In the early 1950s, he was twice Golden Gloves champion of New Mexico. Now he has nothing to do with the tournament mainly, he says, because no one asks for his support. "I wouldn't mind being a trainer. But hey, I don't beg." The immense pride sometimes spills over to outright anger. "This town had no boxing reputation till I gave it one. I brought two championship fights here. And what do I get for it? They'll never be another boxing champion out of Albuquerque."

Bobby Wayne Foster was born in a three-room house on Ellington Drive in the South Valley. The home still stands; Foster's sister lives in it. When he's on patrol, Foster will often drive by both residences: the tiny run-down place on Ellington, and the big fancy ranchhouse with the pool on Harris Drive, a few miles away. Foster says the comparison is good for him.

All Foster remembers of his father, who left home when Bobby was four, was that he was "mean." "If he's still alive, I think I would have heard from him when I was champ." Foster's mother, Bertha, died in 1973. If there was any one event that made him quit the ring it was her death. A maid at the Franciscan Hotel for many years, Bertha Foster was her son's soul, his inner glue. "She taught me a lot about money—that it was the root of all evil. She was right, too."

He learned to box at the Albuquerque Boy's Club, but it was in the Air Force, which he joined at seventeen, that Foster began to carve out a distinguished amateur career. In 1961 he turned pro but had to wait seven years before he got a light heavyweight title bout against Dick Tiger in Madison Square Garden. Foster decked the African in the fourth round.

Undefeated in his weight class, Foster had trouble finding opponents: he is tall—six feet, three and one-half inches. Possessing considerable reach, he fought with an explosive if peculiar laid-low left hand (forty-two knockouts in fifty-two pro fights). To make money, Foster had to take on heavyweights who often outweighed him by twenty-five pounds or more. Gamely, he went against Joe Frazier and Ali during those years, only to be punished. Like Ali and Frazier, Foster's descent seemed to drag on interminably. Just as one thought he was long retired, a small newspaper headline would appear: "Bob Foster To Fight in Bahamas." The foe was apt to be an unknown seeking the same monetary cushion as Foster.

Always wanting to be a police officer, he joined the sheriff's department in 1971. "They treat me good," he says. Foster is known as a conscientious lawman. But still: "It's just that I don't think I belong behind a desk or putting somebody in jail."

The other morning Foster, who usually boxed at 174 pounds, stepped on the scales. "One ninety-seven," he reports. "Most ever. Got to stop eating and drinking." At his height he can take the extra weight. Gone, however, are the days when he used to run nonstop from the Rio Bravo

Bridge to Barelas Bridge and back, six miles. On the rare occasions Foster goes to his old William Street gym, off South Broadway, he will jump rope for five minutes at most, maybe use the big bag a bit. Then his head will begin to pound.

He never watches boxing on television. "Want to hear something funny? I don't even know who's lightheavy champ now." One fighter he does follow is James Scott, a light heavyweight who is serving a fifty-year sentence in a New Jersey prison. A while back Scott wrote Foster for advice. Flattered someone remembered, Foster wrote back. A friendship has developed. "I don't think he'll ever get a shot at the title," says Foster. "Unless somebody can buy his way out of prison like they did with Sonny Liston."

His own financial problems are less severe these days. To restore dignity and self-worth, Foster recently hired a new attorney. The ex-fighter's far from rich, however. "Money's good to have, but you know when I didn't have any I didn't go up to the Sandias and blow my brains out. What's money, anyhow? I see people in this Valley who'd kill you for three dollars."

Mixed emotions about the place have driven Foster from Albuquerque's South Valley. He owns a small house in the Northeast Heights now. When he goes out it's to Legion Post Ninety-Nine, or to the Elks. Mostly he stays home where he watches television or shows a film of one of his fights. "That's the way I like to spend an evening. Maybe drink some Coors, have a V.O." His ex-wife Pearl has the film of the Dick Tiger fight, the big one, and Foster tries not to think about that. He tries not to think about a lot of things—doctor's orders. "Hey, babe, I'm looking ahead, not behind," he says, staring into an empty coffee cup. "Things aren't too bad. They could be a whole lot worse."

Urban Indian

ALBUQUERQUE—The newsroom at KOAT-TV is a broad, noisy chamber. Toward the middle of the room is Conroy Chino's desk. In one sense, the positioning of Chino's work area represents his life right now—a way station amidst urban din. Though that desk is sixty miles from Ácoma Pueblo, Chino's thoughts of his birthplace are always close at hand.

This is a man whose childhood memories hold clues to who he is. Mornings were for hitching up a horse-drawn wagon bound for corn fields; summer afternoons for splashing in a rain-swollen swimming hole; evenings for listening to elderly relatives pass down Ácoma legends. The little sandstone house in McCartys that Conroy Chino was born in twenty-nine years ago, the house he grew up in with nine other children, is now abandoned. Wilbert Chino, Conroy's father and a welder for Kerr-McGee, has moved the family into a contemporary frame home built by the U.S. government.

Nearly 18,000 Indians reside in Albuquerque. Most work for Indian-related services or for large bureaucratic organizations. Conroy Chino is different. He is a reporter for a privately-owned television station. Though he is not, like so many of those 18,000, a stranger in a strange land, he *is* like them: there will forever be a part of Chino that cannot be separated from that stone house.

The distance between poverty-plagued McCartys, New Mexico, and Princeton University, where Chino once worked toward a doctorate, the distance between McCartys and a desk at KOAT-TV even, is formidable, especially when one hears the simple single-word explanation of how that ground was covered—bookmobile. The bookmobile, says Chino, came to McCartys ever month or so. He can recall three early books: *Crazy Horse, PT-109,* and a story about a young Arab boy. Chino grew up a reader, quiet and introspective, and Catholic. At fourteen, he was sent by his mother, Velma, to Santa Barbara, California, to train for the seminary. Chino's ambitions were not with the priesthood; he wanted "excitement and adventure."

If California disciplined his academics, it also threw Chino into angry confusion. He had never been to a non-Indian school and the prejudice within his Jesuit academy was immense. "I was the dumb savage," he says. "I got into a lot of fights because of it."

Returning to the stone house in McCartys during school vacations only clouded his anger. Yes, he saw his parents were poor, that Ácoma was backward. But he also saw a heritage he could not disown. It was only after entering the University of New Mexico in 1968 that Chino's frustrations began to diminish. The various political and antiwar movements on campus galvanized what few Native American students there were. Chino found himself with a group that included a Mescalero, a Santa Claran, a couple of Navajos. Gathering at night in each others' apartments, the students would share experiences. Suddenly it was acceptable to be an Indian, says Chino. "I would go home to McCartys filled with all this rhetoric and say, 'Hey, it's okay to be Ácoma'." Chino's mother and grandmother would look at their son strangely. *Gwee-shu-wah,* they would say, addressing Conroy by his Indian name. *Gwee-shu-wah,* just when were you not Ácoma?

Ácoma people were pleased when Chino went off to Princeton to study for a Ph.D. in English. The program was rigorous, however, and despite feeling more secure about his background, Chino had trouble adjusting. A year in New Jersey and he was back in Albuquerque. For a time he worked in radio. Then, in 1973, he applied for a job at KOAT-TV and was hired. For eleven months Chino was a reporter and cameraman. Some of his stories found their way on the air, including a two-part series on the urban Indian. In Ácoma, Chino became a celebrity. Young, highly educated, and with a bright career before him, in December of 1974 Chino quit KOAT. He was going back to the reservation. Unlike the bookmobile, there is no easy explanation for his returning home. He says it was something he "felt."

Ácoma is made up of several clans. Conroy Chino's clan is Antelope, from his mother's side; much is expected of Antelope members spiritually and in matters of leadership. Because the Antelope clan uncles were getting old, Wilbert and Velma Chino strongly urged their oldest son, Conroy, to return home. Chino says that whatever he might have been doing at that time—broadcast journalist or college professor—he would have forsaken for his homeland.

Welcomed back with open arms, Chino was made tribal secretary. He would be working with the governor, helping mainly with correspondence. Chino felt no bitterness. He was glad, he says, to be where he was. Still, because of his outside exposure, he felt unattached. Perhaps to fasten Ácoma ties that had been loosened, his first year back on the reservation he lived at Old Ácoma, the famed Sky City. Though Sky City is revered as a historic site, few Ácoma Indians live there. Chino's house, owned by his parents, was like all Old Ácoma residences—without running water, electricity, or modern conveniences. "That winter was really rough," Chino says. "But the sense of peacefulness and serenity gave me time to think."

Each night after work Chino would drive home to Sky City, 350 feet atop a mesa. he would sit in his parents' ancient home and try to feel the centuries beneath him. Occasionally he would be visited by his great-grandfather, José Ortiz. Nearly blind and 114 years old when he died, José Ortiz was a farmer with an incredible wealth of oral history. "He would tell me wonderful stories," says Chino. "Great-grandfather was really a link to my past."

During his second year on the reservation, Chino began seeing an Ácoma woman named Darva Randolph. A divorcée, she had a small son, Daaron. Soon Chino moved out of Sky City and into a rented home with Darva and Daaron. Living out of wedlock is greatly frowned upon at Ácoma and Chino knew it. But the year at Sky City had taught him something; though he might be Ácoma, there was another part of him that would be forever different.

Late in 1977 Chino realized it was time to leave Ácoma. As tribal secretary, his term was about to expire, and Darva had taken a job at the Albuquerque Indian School. Again the city called. There is a tradition in Ácoma that says while the young should feel free to seek knowledge, they should return to the reservation. While Chino felt the three years he had given the pueblo were enough, many of the older people, even the ones who once praised his television efforts, did not agree. "They are the conservative ones," Chino says, without rancor. "They are the ones who say, 'This is the way things have always been done'."

To many younger people, however, Chino's departure was applauded. They saw his leaving as a sign of real progress, that the "out there" had relevance, that the urban Indian could make it. Although Chino did not get a chance to tell tribal elders why he needed to leave, he did talk with the then-governor, Stanley Paytiamo. A man Chino greatly admires, Stanley Paytiamo understood. So did Chino's parents, even though Conroy would be the only one of their ten offspring to desert Ácoma. Some months later Chino went back to work at KOAT-TV. Shortly after that he wed Darva Randolph.

Even rebellious people get homesick. Chino's modern Taylor Ranch home is about as far as one can get from Albuquerque, still be within the city's limits, and yet be on the way West, toward his pueblo. "When I contrast the warmth of Ácoma with the city," Chino says, "there is no comparison. I don't even know who lives two houses down from me." He returns to Ácoma for feast days and other religious holidays, but it is this life—this often cold way station—that he has chosen, at least for the moment. Someday, Chino is certain he will go home and build a stone house at McCartys. There is something out there, Chino says, nodding toward the West, and Ácoma. There is something out there that even he, who is supposed to be well-educated, cannot fully explain. "It has to do with personal identity. It goes a long way back."

Mind Reader

LOS ALAMOS—There is a scene in one of Judy Blume's books where a thirteen-year-old boy, surrounded at a dinner table by adults, reflects silently to himself on how a woman becomes pregnant. Stopping to look at the grown-ups around him, the boy suddenly wonders anxiously: *Do they know what I'm thinking?*

It is a small piece of writing, a speck on a single page. Yet it is the kind of moment that has made Judy Blume famous, the kind of perception that causes young readers to send her more than 1,000 letters each month. "Here's a letter," Judy Blume was saying the other day. Her voice, like her face, is small and cheerful. The letter, like most this forty-year-old writer receives, concerns a Blume character. "Dear Judy," it begins. "I thought I was the only one with a problem like that. . . ."

Over the past decade, Judy Blume's name has emerged as synonymous with Young Adult Literature. Indeed, Blume books have become a publishing phenomenon. In paperback, they have sold more than six million copies. *Deenie,* written less than five years ago, is in its tenth printing. It is not rare to find youngsters of all sizes badgering mothers in bookstores to purchase a Blume—any Blume—from the rows at hand. "As fast as her books are checked in," says an Albuquerque public librarian, "they're checked out."

Delicately attractive, Judy Blume looks like the schoolgirl who might have been found quietly watercoloring flowers in a corner. She looks like she might have been the only one in the class to know how to spell *accommodate*. She *is* those people. She's also Tony Miglione, a boy whose best friend is a shoplifter. She's Deenie Fenner, an adolescent girl in a body brace who must face her boyfriend's advances. She's Margaret Simon, almost twelve, and overly concerned with how her body is changing; Jill Brenner, tormentor of an overweight classmate; Peter Warren Hatcher, bugged by an obnoxious little brother.

"My readers identify with the people I write about," the author says, "and I identify with each character." Judy Blume is talking from an outdoor cedar balcony at her Los Alamos home. She has lived in Los Alamos for two years, ever since she married Tom Kitchens, a physicist. She likes her hilltop view, but not much else, she admits. Los Alamos is a pleasant town, she says, but too isolated, "too scientific" for her writing. "I don't really get my inspiration from places. I get it from people. I'm a great people-watcher. I need to go down to Santa Fe and just sit in the Plaza."

The writing started in suburban New Jersey when she was a housewife with two small children and time on her hands. "I was frustrated, I guess, and needed something new in my life." First came some imitation Dr. Seuss books and with them lots of rejection slips. "I used to go to bed at night really depressed. 'If only someone would publish me,' I would cry. I didn't even care about being paid." Finally, in 1969, a picture book—*The One in the Middle is the Green Kangaroo*—was published. She didn't get paid much because it sold "maybe ten copies." That was followed by *Iggie's House,* better, but still unsatisfying to the author. "For my third book, I sat down and said, 'Now we're going to write something from the guts'." Out poured *Are You There, God? It's Me, Margaret.* Its appearance turned up a regiment of readers who immediately related to a young girl's intensely personal gropings with menstruation, bra buying, and boys.

A string of novels succeeded *Margaret,* all "from the guts": *Blubber; Deenie; Starring Sally J. Freedman as Herself; Then Again, Maybe I Won't; Tales of a Fourth Grade Nothing.* Then came *Forever,* a sexually explicit look at two high school seniors. It was her first young adult work and sold more than five million copies. When *Forever* became a television movie, scads of parents asked, Who is Judy Blume, anyway? It was their children who told them.

Many of the letters Ms. Blume receives inquire where she gets her ideas. The people she watches most—her family, her friends, and herself—provide much material. From her first marriage, to John Blume, an attorney, she has two children, both of whom live with her: a girl, Randy, seventeen; and Larry, fifteen. *Blubber* came from Randy's being locked in a school coat closet. There are bits of Larry in *Then Again, Maybe I Won't. Deenie,* which is about scoliosis, grew from a cocktail party conversation; *Sally J. Freedman,* from a long-ago vacation to Miami Beach; *Margaret,* from sixth grade memories. "I am what I am because of everything that has happened to me," Ms. Blume frequently tells curious correspondents.

Her childhood was nothing out of the ordinary. It's her recall of it that is important. Ms. Blume clearly remembers everything, right down to the color of the dress she wore on the third-to-last day of school in the fifth grade. She read Nancy Drew books, but is glad her own children didn't. At twelve or thirteen, she began poking into her parents' book collection. "I read *The Fountainhead* before I knew what Ayn Rand was really talking about. You know, I was looking for a phrase that might stand out. I found it, all right, about a man biting a woman's breast. Later, I read the book for the story."

As a teenager, she wanted to be a wife and a mother, maybe president of the PTA. "Those were 1950s ideas. You go to college and graduate with a degree in education in case, God forbid, you had to work someday. Your big job in college was to find the right husband." After sixteen years of marriage, she divorced Mr. Right. She met Tom Kitchens on a plane flight from Denver to Tulsa.

The divorce, the second marriage, the move to New Mexico have been tough at times on her children, she says. "But no kid has it easy today. There are so many decisions to make. That's the point of my writing. Kids today have to cope with parents' choices. When I was growing up, I didn't know anybody who lived with divorced parents. I don't think life up until junior high has changed that much since I was a kid, but high school certainly has. There are so many pressures—booze, drugs, sex—all available in the school parking lot. I'm amazed at how many letters I get from ten-year-olds about *Forever*."

Because Ms. Blume writes graphically (the main character in *Deenie,* for instance, masturbates), she draws her share of criticism. When *Margaret* was published, its author excitedly rushed three copies to her own children's school library in New Jersey. An irate parent had the books removed. The incident still rankles her: "Adults are way off base when they think how something might influence a teenager. Books can be used as bridges between parent and child. You can't protect a child from the real world forever." Occasionally she gets chastised for not trying to make that real world better. This angers her. "In my personal life, I'm wildly romantic. But in my books, I refuse to give in; I'm frank. The trouble with romance is that it stands in the way of real-life."

A reviewer once labeled her the Jacqueline Susann of children's literature. To be reminded of the comment causes Judy Blume's eyes to roll in bewilderment. "I write about what I like to think children are interested in, what they're feeling. Young kids really want to know what a man and a woman do to each other. They want to know without it being sordid."

For the past three years Ms. Blume has sacrificed her ideas about what children think about, to work on her first adult novel, *Wifey*. It's the story of a wife, naturally, from suburban New Jersey, naturally. "I'm frightened to death of this book," she reveals. "My agent knows, my editor knows, and I know, that we're probably going to take a beating from reviewers. But it was a book I had to write. The adult tone was hard to capture, even though the book's characters are childlike adults. What's the book about? A wife who doesn't slam the door on her marriage, who doesn't walk off. Her husband is a clod and a creep, but human." Judy Blume pauses to giggle. "The book's got a lot of sex in it." Naturally.

Since this article appeared, the following have occurred: Judy Blume and her husband have moved to Santa Fe; Wifey *received cool reviews; and its author has returned to writing books for young adults.*

Shu-pac Operator

ALBUQUERQUE—It is mid-morning and I am riding in the seat that in my youth was jeeringly referred to as the spot held down by one's closest female relatives: shotgun on a garbage truck. Alongside me is the vehicle's driver, Noe Chavez. We are traveling in the Southeast Heights, somewhere between Carlisle Boulevard and Ridgecrest Drive, just exactly where I'm not sure since every time I look up we make a turn.

"The hardest part of this job is running a route," Chavez is telling me. "Anybody can pick up garbage. On a route, though, you don't want to backtrack. You don't want to go down the same street twice the same way." Because Chavez hops on and off the right side of his truck, he tries to make as many right-hand turns as possible. Heuristic routing, it's called. It takes practice.

When there's only one bag on the curb I stay put and stare at Chavez's window visor, which is decorated with a crucifix and a key chain. When there's more than one bag I make an effort to help out. In the last hour I've discovered not just anybody can pick up garbage.

For each of the four days he works, Noe Chavez (he pronounces his first name *No-ay*) has four different routes. As a week progresses, he moves from west to east. Mondays he's on the West Mesa; Thursdays, it's Four Hills. Like all Albuquerque drivers, Chavez goes alone. Even though I'm sure my presence is slowing him down this day, Chavez says he is glad to have me along.

About five feet, seven inches tall, Noe Chavez has long sideburns, short, thick fingers, and the shoulders of a hod carrier. He is dressed in the uniform of the Albuquerque Refuse Service: a chocolate-colored jump suit, with a gold and red emblem on the left shirt pocket. On his head is a Toyota ball cap. Officially, the city does not call Chavez a garbage collector, nor is he euphemistically known as a sanitation engineer, a solid waste retriever, or even a garbologist. Rather, he goes by the curious label of "Shu-pac operator." The name derives from the truck used on Albuquerque's residential garbage routes. This vehicle features a mechanical rammer blade that pushes and packs hopper-fed trash into a large back compartment. Chavez's big, blue rig is one of forty-two Shu-pacs operating in the city. His vehicle weighs 26,000 pounds empty and will carry up to ten tons of garbage. It costs $66,000 new.

The year 1972 was a zenith in Albuquerque garbage annals. That was the year the city inaugurated both Shu-pacs and curbside plastic garbage bags. Before then, a variety of means was used to gather trash. The most recent method was small, rear-loading trucks manned by a driver and two to three crew members. Those are known in refuse parlance as "trash-by-the-barrel" days. It was an era when a garbage collector went up to a home and emptied one or more cans in a big barrel, lifted that barrel over his shoulder, and then lugged it back to the street. Noe Chavez, who has been a collector fourteen years, remembers that period well. "You had more dog bites then," he says, making a heuristic turn. "You got a lot dirtier, too. Lard, smelly old grass cuttings would get all over you. In the morning, people got mad when you woke them up. No way I want to go back to those days."

While plastic bags have made things easier all around, problems still exist. Some householders, Chavez says, don't bother to tie up the bags. Others block the bags with parked cars. Still others stuff the bags with dead animals or fireplace ashes. When Noe Chavez picks up a garbage bag filled with ashes, and he doesn't know it's ashes, and then throws that bag into his hopper, there's a good chance the Shu-pac's rammer blade will break the bag and Chavez will end up with a face full of soot. What occurs when a bag containing a dead animal breaks doesn't bear describing.

Although the switch to Shu-pacs cut costs, it has nearly wiped out personal contact. In the past, a garbage man's proximity to a home often created familiarity between collector and resident. That seldom happens anymore. "I know a few people now," says Chavez. "Not many." Making rounds with Chavez I notice an occasional "garbage groupie" waiting for our truck. There'll be a good-morning greeting, maybe talk about the weather. Invariably these persons will help Chavez hoist an item or two. Most people, though, do not even look at us. A few come out the front door to gingerly hand over a bag held between thumb and forefinger—as if the contents were a bomb, or worse yet, *gahr-baaawge*. Pulling up to a box of empty wine and beer bottles causes Chavez to smile ruefully. "You get to know a lot about people collecting garbage. You get to know who drinks and how much. You see sloppy garbage and you think maybe people inside that house are sloppy."

As with death and taxes, there's an inevitability about garbage. And if you live in Albuquerque, there's a certainty you will be billed four dollars monthly, whether you choose or not to set out rubbish. Every Albuquerquean by himself produces roughly three and one-half pounds of garbage a day. Fifty to sixty percent of it is paper: junk mail, letters from Aunt Gladys, egg cartons, and milk containers. The rest is as follows: lawn and garden waste (ten percent); food waste (nine percent); glass and ceramics (eight and one-half percent); metal (seven and one-half percent); rags, plastic, rubber, and leather (six percent).

We come to a home with a battered laundry hamper on the sidewalk. "You're not supposed to take anything over seventy-five pounds," Chavez says. "I'll take things heavier; I'll take things up to five feet long, if there's someone around who'll help me put them into the truck. Lots of people don't want to help. They'll say, 'Well, that's what we're paying you for.' You can't argue."

Plentiful are the stories of one man's castoffs becoming another's treasures. I ask Chavez if he's experienced any discoveries. "We're not supposed to keep anything that's left out front, but a lot of drivers do. They'll take it to the dump, hide it there, and come back for it later." Chavez admits to keeping a broken tricycle. He took it home and in minutes had it fixed for his five-year-old son. His best find was a nineteen-inch color television set. "All it needed was the dials to be tightened."

For years I've heard rumors about the extravagant salaries earned by garbage men. All Albuquerque drivers make seven dollars and nineteen cents an hour, for a forty-hour week. "Back when I started it was a buck and a quarter and we worked twice as hard," Chavez says. "Now we only work four days and go home when we finish our route."

Born thirty-six years ago in Alameda, New Mexico, Chavez still lives near there with his wife, Edwina, three children, two cows, and a rabbit. He dropped out of Albuquerque High School in the eleventh grade to take a job as a dishwasher. Later, he did construction, plastering, and yard work until he joined the Job Corps. That led to a tryout with the Albuquerque Refuse Service. "For the first two weeks I wanted to quit every day. I would come home and just lie down." In those days of four-person crews, older hands would see to it that a new man like Chavez was given "heavy" streets. Neighborhoods are still categorized in terms of trash volume. They're either heavy or light. "Four Hills is heavy," Chavez says. The Generals—General Stilwell, General Arnold, General Bradley, and so forth in Albuquerque's Northeast Heights, are also considered heavy.

Nomenclature is part of the picture. A garbage truck is a *unit.* "You got to keep your unit clean," Chavez says. "You got to check your own oil and everything each morning. If your unit breaks down, you still got to finish your route." On any route there might be a *header,* or a street, usually a circular drive or a cul-de-sac, with only a few garbage bags. Nobody likes headers, according to Chavez. "They slow you down." Failure to pick up a header may result in a "1035," or a complaint, also to be avoided. "You can't win a 1035," Chavez notes. "The public is always right."

There are more: a substitute driver is an *extra board.* An accident investigation is a *fact-finding.* A commercial garbage truck is a *roll-off.* Wintertime is the best time to work, Chavez feels. In the summer, kids roam the streets, there's more traffic, the truck gets hot and so does the garbage. The worse thing about summer is the nasty little white garbage bugs that infest truck and bag. The insects are known in the trade as *walking rice.*

Standing sentinel at a two-story home is a mountain of odds and ends: tires, shopping bags full of old dishes, stacks of magazines. I swing down out of the truck to lend a hand. "These people are moving," Chavez announces. "When people move in or out it's always heavy."

As we hurl debris toward the truck's hopper, Chavez tells me that when he was little he wanted to be a policeman. "My father? He worked for Sandia Base for thirty-five years. No, he doesn't think anything about what I do. See, I have a job and I do it. My little boy, he wants to drive a truck like me. I would rather he go to school." Seniority has placed Chavez in line for a management post. But he's not sure he wants to do anything else. "This is a good job," he remarks, tapping the side of his truck. That he might possibly be aiding the environment has nothing to do with his feelings. His job is simply a *good* one. Says Chavez, "You get used to it."

We come to a large white house with tweezer-cut lawn and a trapezoidal swimming pool. "That guy may have money," Chavez observes. "He's still got bills, no?" I ask Chavez if he ever feels embarrassed by what he does. He shakes his head, then explains: "Like in summer, you'll see kids sitting on the park bench. When I drive by they'll hold their nose. That kind of thing doesn't bother me. Someone's got to do this work." I ask him if he knows any garbageman jokes. A bit uncomfortably Chavez says he doesn't, not even the answer to this age-old teaser: What has four wheels and flies? (Chavez's unit, I later learn, has ten wheels.)

I glance at my wristwatch. It is 12:30 P.M. We have worked four and one-half hours nonstop and serviced 550 homes. Now we are done. Chavez's workday began at 8:00 A.M. in the City Yard, south of Coronado Airport. Normally, he makes two trips to the dump each route and is finished by 2:00 P.M. This day, only one dumping is needed. Most of the streets have been light.

On our way to the dump, Chavez speaks again of the

physical aspects of the job. "Anybody can pick up garbage," he repeats. And yet I sense he believes this not quite true, especially when he reveals the following: "Once I trained a guy who was six feet tall and weighed 220 pounds. He had arms out to here. But he kept sweating all the time. After a while he just couldn't take it. When you can't do this job anymore they send you to Weed and Litter Patrol."

By 1:00 P.M. we have arrived at the dump, otherwise known as a landfill. A deep wide cavity that resembles a volcanic crater, the landfill is not far from City Yard. At the basin of this chasm I watch as Chavez pushes a button that raises and then tips his trash compartment backward. Out spill eggshells, worn-out shoes, last year's calendars, last night's half-eaten TV dinners, and bags and bags and bags of life's jetsam. "Tired?" Chavez asks. I nod. I haven't worked anywhere near the amount he has, yet my body feels like it might have been sent through a Shu-pac hopper. I mention this. Chavez smiles, then says, "You get used to it."

Mountain Goat

JEMEZ MOUNTAINS—The route east from State Highway 4 to the steep canyons is marked by clammy, red earth, the kind of soil that sticks to car tires. People from the area warn that if you hike up into this lung-searing land, you will have muddy shoes and be out of breath within minutes. Should you decide to run up, they say, you are nuts. "Only one person runs these mountains," brags a clerk at the Jemez Ranger Station. "That's Aloysius."

Sunlight is waning as Aloysius Waquie climbs out of a pea green Chevrolet pickup and touches the red dirt with his fingertips. A wisp of a man, Al Waquie is five feet, three inches and 117 pounds—on a good day. His eyes are dark and miss little, his complexion in the fading dusk, that of fried bacon. "I feel great," says Waquie, patting where his white T-shirt meets his purple sweat pants at a nearly nonexistent stomach. "I think I'll do this run three times tonight," he announces as he pushes off effortlessly, his blue running shoes lightly massaging the slope beneath him.

Three times up and down these mountains is more than most people would care to attempt. But then, Al Waquie

(Wah-kee) devours inclines the way some people do pistachio nuts. "King of the Hills," he's called, at least in New Mexico. "I don't know what it is," Waquie says of his passion for running up hills. "The higher I go the better I feel." For the last two years Waquie has finished first in the nationally-recognized La Luz Trail Run, a humbling seven and one-half mile trek up the west face of Albuquerque's Sandia Peak. Last year, Waquie shattered his own La Luz record of an hour flat (he did fifty-seven minutes and forty seconds) and in doing so beat his closest challenger by an astonishing four minutes. So overwhelming a favorite is Waquie in the La Luz that one entrant concedes, "Al owns the race. Everybody will be running for second."

As usual, Waquie is not so sure. "People tell me so-and-so is working out this year. That just makes me train harder." It was fifteen years ago, when Waquie was thirteen, that he entered his first race, a four-miler over the roads near his Jemez Pueblo home. Without a lick of training he came in fourth in a field of twenty-two. His finish was not all that surprising. Al Waquie comes from a long line of runners. His grandfather Felipé, his father Felix, his brothers Stanley and Robert, are all runners. Years ago Felipé and Felix used to chase wild horses across the plains west of the pueblo. Sometimes they would be gone five days. Felipé also served as a pueblo messenger, traveling twenty miles over the mountains to Santo Domingo Pueblo.

Waquie has five brothers and three sisters. Enormously modest about his own abilities, he is unimpressed with the running skills of his siblings. "My brother José, he runs every night, but he's not too good. My brother Sal, he doesn't run at all. Well, he did run a mile the other day." Not until his junior year in high school did Waquie begin to concentrate on running. As a sophomore he was sixth man on the cross country team. Two years later he was the state's Class B champion. After a year at Western New Mexico University in Silver City, Waquie transferred to Haskell Indian Junior College in Lawrence, Kansas, where he made all-America in cross country.

Because he had always played baseball in the spring, disdaining track, Waquie had never run around an oval until he arrived at Haskell. The track coach there decided to clock him in the mile, and Waquie did a respectable four minutes and twenty-six seconds. With a little work, the coach said, Waquie could be in the teens. No, Al replied, he was not a miler. "I don't like anything that goes round and round. I'd rather go in a straight line."

What he would really rather do, he discovered, was go uphill—way, way up. When he left junior college, Waquie returned to the Jemez area and went to work for the Forest Service, still his employer. A forestry technician on a thinning crew, he spends most of his day at extremely high altitudes wrestling an eight-pound chain saw. It is bone-wearying work, not the type of activity that would normally leave one wanting much more afterward. Each evening though, Waquie heads for the hills around Jemez Pueblo, mountains he has known since he was a boy who went hunting in them with his father. He almost always runs alone—in the Gilman area, over the Peggy Mesa, through the mesas around tiny Canyon, New Mexico. Once he knew the names of all the mesas, but now he has forgotten most. Not that his Indian heritage is unimportant; in the pueblo, Waquie holds the title of War Captain, a duty which requires him to recruit dancers for the special ceremonies throughout the year.

A bachelor, Waquie says he feels no guilt giving so much free time to the mountains. Relentless workouts are a pleasure—to be relished for their solitude. This is *his* land. "I got trails marked hardly anybody but me knows about." He does his speed work up there, sprinting abandoned logging roads as fast as he can; or he takes long, loping runs at 9,400 feet, jogs that can last up to two and a half hours. Along the way he'll often see elk or deer and occasionally will pursue one or the other. His endurance once permitted him to catch up with a buck. During one workout last year Waquie saw a bear; he did not give chase.

As he runs this evening in his quirky but loose upright style, Waquie spots some footprints. He smiles. These are Steven Gachupin's tracks, he says. Far ahead, a lonely figure on the mountain moves slowly—Steven Gachupin. A Jemez Indian in his mid-thirties, Gachupin is also something of a La Luz Trail Run legend. In the late 1960s, Gachupin won La Luz four consecutive times, something no one else has done. In 1970, Gachupin finished second, and thereafter began a downward slide. He is past his prime now, this Jemez Valley School janitor, and more than likely will never be a factor again. Waquie knows this but there is respect in his voice when he catches sight of Gachupin: Al Waquie has won La Luz but twice.

Actually, Waquie should have three victories. In his first La Luz in 1976, he came in second to Rick Trujillo, of Colorado. "I got psyched out," Waquie says. "Everybody at the start kept telling me how great Trujillo was." Believing them, Waquie refused to challenge the Coloradoan and at the summit nearly slowed to a trot. Trujillo won by four seconds. "I've been looking for him again," says Waquie of Trujillo. "But he hasn't come back." Waquie has also awaited Arizona's Chuck Smith, considered by many to be America's premier hill runner. But Smith, also apparently avoiding Waquie, has never entered the La Luz. Smith has run the Pikes Peak Hill Climb and holds the course record there. Waquie has never run Pikes Peak. And that may be part of the problem, if indeed it is a problem. Although he wins most local races, Waquie is nearly unknown outside his own state. Quite possibly he has the gifts to do well elsewhere, but he has never tried. Some believe that if he did have a coach, if he did have someone to push him to train harder, someone to coax him to sign up for more prestigious hill races around the country, that perhaps Al Waquie's heart might not be in it.

Certainly Waquie would welcome the extra competition; he no longer fears other runners. But there is something about him that seems to say win-at-all-costs running, done on a broad scale, is not really worth it. While other runners seem consumed with recording daily wind direction, food intake and the like, such data are completely foreign to Waquie. Asked what his resting pulse rate is, Waquie says he has no idea.

That Waquie enjoys running purely for fun is perhaps best exemplified by something he did just recently. He ran La Luz for practice, holding a stopwatch in one hand. He ran it, he says, because it was a "nice day." His time of sixty-one minutes and thirty-one seconds would have placed him second last year. "When I got to 8,000 feet, I was barely breathing hard," he reports of the practice outing. This year's La Luz will be set on a longer course, more than nine miles. The additional two miles has Waquie worried; it's not the extra yardage that bothers him, but the fact that it is mostly on flat ground. *"The higher I go...."*

To cheer Waquie on, a large contingent from Jemez Pueblo will be at the La Luz finish line for this year's race. Friends from high school, Forest Service co-workers, baseball buddies, all will address Waquie by any number of names: *Lurch, or Weege, or Goat* (as in mountain) and, of course, Aloysius. Aloysius seems fitting: a late sixteenth century Italian Jesuit, St. Aloysius, the patron of youth, led a life of severe penance.

Al Waquie has gone on to win two more La Luz Trail Runs since this appeared. Additionally, he has finally ventured out-of-state, and set a course record at a run up Pikes Peak.

4: Celebrators

"I do think we're upgradin' the folks down there."

The Game

ELIDA—A small village in one of Anton Chekhov's short stories is made memorable to those who pass by and ask what village it is when they're told, "That's the one where the deacon ate up all the caviar at the funeral." Of Elida, and of nearby Floyd, two New Mexico pindot communities nearly as interchangeable as butter and margarine, travelers tend to be informed, "That's where they play basketball." In Elida, or twenty-one miles northeast in Floyd, football doesn't exist. The basketball season, scheduled or otherwise, runs August-to-August. And when Elida High School goes against Floyd High, when butter meets margarine, it's always "The Game."

Because records are incomplete, nobody knows how many times The Game has been played. What people do know is that it's not been played enough. On the strength of some dandy teams in the 1930s and 1940s, Floyd probably has won The Game more. In 1935, when no divisions existed in state tournament play, little Floyd won the New Mexico high school championship.

There are many who believe the rivalry stems from the

two towns being so much alike. Named for a settler who had daughters named Ella and Ida, Elida was founded in 1902. The town is older than Floyd—by less than six months. With a population of 300, Floyd is slightly smaller than Elida. Both high schools have approximately eighty students. And both towns have three churches: Baptist, Methodist, and Church of Christ. Perhaps the greatest difference between the two places is how their residents earn a living. Elida is mainly a ranching community, while most folks in Floyd farm. "It's the water over there," sniffs a Floyd cattle man. "They got irrigation." (Floyd is 345 feet lower in elevation.) Some say farming, and the physical rigors it involves, has given Floyd a distinct advantage through the years—invariably the town comes up with taller boys. But by and large what makes the game The Game is that the inhabitants of the two towns *know* one another. Not just well, but often intimately, and so it seems true that familiarity breeds contempt.

It's 2:20 P.M. on Friday afternoon in the Elida gymnasium. It is five hours until The Game and a pep rally is in progress. "We're number one! They're number two!" shouts Elida Tiger cheerleader Lisa May. "We're gonna knock the———out of you!" Sitting on the bottom step of the bleachers and watching grimly is Elida's coach, Ted Radcliff. Fair-haired and twenty-eight, Radcliff is an integral part of The Game. He grew up on an Elida ranch and played for the Tigers (class of Sixty-nine). After college at Eastern New Mexico University, and a coaching stint in Arizona, Radcliff crossed enemy lines and accepted a job as head basketball coach for the Floyd High School Broncos.

"Let me tell you it was the most awful year of my life," Radcliff drawls. "We won fourth in the state, first time in ten years they'd been to state. But I got nothing but headaches." Radcliff says he came to hate Floyd, even more than when he was an Elida student. "The kids were an uppity bunch when I was coaching over there. Every time I tried to do something they'd cross me, or else their parents would." Toward the middle of his first year at Floyd, after countless showdowns with school board members, Radcliff was told his contract would not be renewed. For a year and a half he drove a truck in Portales. He vowed he would never coach again. Then Elida called. It took Radcliff four months to say yes. Though he is on his home turf now, Radcliff knows he isn't yet out of the woods. "Come contract time, no matter what my record, the school board here will look to see if we've beaten Floyd."

It's 3:35 P.M. and a group of Elida students is hanging around the Sixty-six Cafe ("Home-style chili and beans, $1.75"), waiting for a bus that will take them to Floyd and The Game. Jeff Bilberry, a Tiger forward, leans back in a chair and sips a Dr. Pepper. Bilberry thinks of The Game in fairly friendly terms: his grandparents, an uncle, and two cousins live in Floyd. "My Dad went to school there but my mother went to Elida. Yessir, they'll be rooting for Elida." Bilberry's teammate Joel Nuckols says he can recall a couple of fights between the two schools. "There'll be a lot of elbowing and clawing and some cuss words on that court tonight," says Nuckols who, like his father and uncle before him, is a veteran of The Game.

No matter how amiable a contest professes to be, there comes a time when participants must choose between winning and goodwill. For Elida and Floyd, that moment came in 1965. Greg Burris, a star senior player for Elida, got married that year. Because Elida then had a rule prohibiting married students from attending school, Greg's parents looked around for another center of learning. For a basketball family, there was really only one other place to go; the Burris clan rented a trailer in Floyd. That season, thanks to Greg Burris's thirty-two points per game average, Floyd finished with a twenty-seven and one record. More than fifteen years later, the Burris affair (the family eventually moved back to Elida) is for many Tiger fans a canker that will not heal.

Four-fifteen P.M. Thirty-year-old Dwayne Kibbe, the Floyd coach, is resting his chubby body on a hideaway sofa in his small home close by Floyd High School. As Ted Radcliff did, Kibbe grew up on an Elida ranch, went to school there, and graduated from ENMU. Hired originally as the girls' coach, Kibbe came to Floyd the same year as Radcliff, and was made boys' coach when Radcliff left. "Heck," says Kibbe. "I've known Ted all my life. We used to rope calves together." Floyd people feel the chief distinction between the two men is that Ted Radcliff never learned how to play the game. (Not The Game, for the year Radcliff coached Floyd his Broncos split with Elida, but the game of not rocking the boat.) Kibbe says to play the game a small-town basketball coach needs to be a politician. "You walk into the store here and a parent will corner you and say, 'Why isn't Johnny playing?' You've got to give him an answer he can accept. Ted's problem here was that he was too outspoken, too blunt. If a boy couldn't play worth a nickel, Ted would tell the boy's daddy just that."

According to Kibbe, the pressures of small-town coaching are large. "You're being watched closely in a place like this. The school is such a vital part of the parents's lives. You get instant feedback on anything you do here." The strain has caught up with Kibbe—he has recently taken up smoking. "I can't guarantee you what's going to happen tonight," Kibbe says, lighting a cigarette. "When we play Elida anything goes and usually does. I heard that a few years back a Floyd parent ran out of the stands and hit an Elida player. Caused quite an eruption. I can tell you one thing, though. Our season's made if we beat Elida."

Five twenty-five P.M. Fifty yards from Kibbe's home, Howard Wright, principal of Floyd High School, is setting up the gym's concession stand. The fifty-year-old Wright is from Roswell and has been at Floyd two years, long enough to know what basketball means to rural Roosevelt County. Wright says he is certain some Floyd parents would be willing to sacrifice just about anything in the school's curriculum before doing anything that might hurt the Bronco basketball program. Wright also has come to know the intensity of The Game. After viewing his first Elida-Floyd battle, a contest Floyd won by eight points, Wright remembers talking to a Floyd school board member. "I was all excited and expected the man to be too," says Wright. "But he just looked at me and said, real sour-like, 'I'd just as soon we had doubled their score'."

Five forty-two P.M. As he's done nearly every game since graduating from Floyd High in "Nineteen and fifty," Wendell Best is easing his long frame behind the gym's tiny scorer's table. It is fitting that Wendell Best should keep score. Few people in Floyd have more influence. Best is president of the school board. His father-in-law is R. C. (Ike) Morgan, longtime linchpin of the New Mexico state senate, and a Bronco of the mid-1920s. Three of Best's children played for Floyd. The Lord willing, Best says his ten-year-old boy, Kyle, will someday be a Bronco.

More than anyone, Wendell Best was responsible for the firing of Ted Radcliff. Best insists there are no hard feelings. "I've known Ted all my life. Our families rodeoed together. Ted just couldn't get along here." Best also declares there is no bad blood between Floyd and Elida; only a healthy, across-the-pasture urge to come out on top. Why, Best gets his mail in Elida, as many Floyd denizens do and vice versa. Why, Best's daughter, Barbara, is married to an Elida boy, Bob Rogers. Why, lots and lots of Floyd people go marrying Elida people. "Course when that happens," Best explains, "I do think we're upgradin' the folks down there."

Five-fifty P.M. A small coterie is beginning to file out of Dunc Fuqua's country store and cafe ("Jumbo cheeseburger, $1.55"), across the street from Floyd High. Though most of those departing Dunc's farm for a living, with Elida in town who can talk soybeans?

Five fifty-seven P.M. Floyd's gym is a pond of Stetson hats and feed-brand gimme caps. The gym itself is a new building. Its hardwood floors gleam and its cream and yellow walls sparkle. Floyd citizens are enormously proud of their modern athletic facility, so proud it appears, that Elida has begun a school building project of its own. The new Floyd gym was sorely needed. A few years back the Broncos played Cimarron in what might be legitimately termed a barn-burner. An electrical short during the second quarter caused the old gym to burn to the ground. "Lots of people around Floyd," grumps Ted Radcliff, "still think I was responsible for that fire."

Nine thirty-five P.M. There were no fights this night. No fires, either. There was plenty of action, though; nearly all of Elida's starters fouled out. At one point the referee called time and scolded Dwayne Kibbe for excessive yelling. When that happened, Ted Radcliff peered down the sideline toward his boyhood friend and, for the first time all day, smiled. It looked for all the world like the smile of someone who just might be learning to play the game. Radcliff's happiness was short-lived. His Elida Tigers lost, fifty to forty-one.

In the parking lot afterward, the outcome of The Game revealed itself in several ways. Floyd principal Howard Wright jubilantly shook hands all around. Elida cheerleader Lisa May, she of the pep rally promises, wiped away tears. Two students—one from Floyd and one from Elida—got into a shoving match. It was broken up finally when the participants were reminded there were chores to be done in the morning. In Elida and in Floyd, everyone has morning chores.

Picture Perfect

HERNANDEZ—It was a late afternoon in the final days of 1941 when a little, bearded man in a floppy hat arrived at this tiny, mountain village six miles northwest of Española. Nobody remembers seeing the man, not even the then thirteen-year-old Annie Roybal, who was helping her father pick onions fifty yards away. Above the Roybal farm, on the highway's crest, the gent in the odd cap stayed but a few minutes—long enough to record what has become one of the most celebrated photographs in the world. The photographer was Ansel Adams. Today, a print of his *Moonrise, Hernandez, New Mexico,* brings $20,000, easily making it one of the most expensive photographs in the world.

To find out what one of the most unlikely-to-be-world-famous spots thinks of all this, you go to "Reggie's," a combination general store and Hernandez hangout. "My son showed me that picture sometime back," says Pat Martinez, leaning against the store's cash register. Martinez is principal of the Hernandez Elementary School. "That picture, it's one of a kind. You can't get another like it. Wasn't it in

Newsweek?" Filiberto Martinez is seventy-two and seemingly like everyone else in this settlement, a cousin to Pat Martinez. In 1941 Filiberto was selling dry goods in Española. "I couldn't pay for that photograph then," he says. "I couldn't pay for it now. Who cares. It's a great honor for us." Annie Roybal has grown up to become Annie Borrego. "My sister showed me that picture," Mrs. Borrego says. "It's so nice it makes me homesick. Wasn't it in *Time* magazine?"

Like most who live in Hernandez, the two Martinez men and Mrs. Borrego were born in the town. Hernandez has changed since the trio was young. In fact, Ansel Adams, strong conservationist that he is, might not want to know the present-day community. In Adams's photograph, Hernandez has a serene look. Bulldozers and monstrous graders belonging to Rio Arriba County now cover vacant lots. Abandoned car hulks dot back yards. Empty oil cans and shredded beer cartons ornament the mud streets.

Hernandez crouches in a valley where the Rio Chama greets the Rio Grande. It was and still is a farming region. Chili, corn, onions and cabbage are chief crops. Hernandez is poor but rich in one important way: no one who lives there seems to resent that the photograph of the town is well-known and the inhabitants are not.

For years photo historians have attributed 1944 as the date of *Moonrise*. In a telephone interview from his home in Carmel, California, Ansel Adams refutes this. "I'm not that good on dates, but I know it was 1941. It had to be." Born in 1902, Adams had already established himself as a photographic genius by 1941. The year before he helped create a photography department at the Museum of Modern Art in New York. He remains an artist, a visionary with a wondrous eye for detail.

In November of 1941, Adams was visiting Santa Fe as

he often did. One sparkling day he and a couple of companions journeyed north to the Chama Valley for some picture taking. "I was battling a stump up there," the photographer remembers. "The stump won. Disgusted, I said, 'Let's go home'." Motoring south on U.S. 84, Adams glanced to his left, toward the east and the snow-covered Truchas peaks. Perched above a classic Hispanic church, graveyard and handful of homes, was a vivid, three-day-full moon. The tableau stirred Adams. "My immediate reaction was 'this is extraordinary'." He nearly ran his wood-panelled Pontiac station wagon into a ditch bank before stopping—just across the highway from where Pat Martinez's grade school now sits.

Knowing he was witnessing something magnificent, Adams tried not to panic, even when he couldn't find his exposure meter. While a tripod was set up on the car's roof, the photographer readied his big view camera—the old bellowslike box instrument—with eight-by-ten Isopan film. Meanwhile, the sun behind him was fading. Adams's ungainly equipment didn't help matters: to operate a view camera one has to close down the lens, put in a film holder, pull out one side of that slide, then put back in the other side. Adams has always been known as a prepared photographer, a technician who leaves nothing to chance. Minus an exposure meter was no hindrance: "The light from the moon offered 250 candles per square foot of luminance." Taking that bit of arcane data into consideration, and the green filter he had attached, Adams made some rapid calculations and released the shutter. "I knew I had a picture." He also knew he had to have another. Back in went the view camera's film holder. Then, in just a matter of seconds, something happened. "The light went off the crosses [in the village cemetery]. The whole scene went dead." So Adams got but the one photograph.

In the early days of its existence the picture was titled *Moonrise Over Hernandez, New Mexico*. Later, the "Over" was dropped. Now it's frequently referred to as simply *Moonrise*. For decades *Moonrise* was just another stunning piece in Ansel Adams's portfolio. Its creator has always like it, but no more than others he's taken. "They're all like favorite children," he says. Beaumont Newhall, the distinguished photographic historian at the University of New Mexico, and a longtime confidant of Adams, doesn't particularly think of *Moonrise* as his friend's best work. "What makes it good, though," says Newhall, "is that it's emotional."

If *Moonrise* has a dominant feature it is its intense values: the pancake clouds hanging from an inky sky. But it is the moon—a veiny omniscient orb—that makes the photograph, that gives it its beguiling mood. There seems to be something almost spiritual about that moon, and Adams agrees. "I think it shows that sometimes we really do have the Lord with us."

For thirty years the price of a *Moonrise* floated between $100 and $200, depending upon the size of the print. In 1975, Adams decided to stop making prints of any negatives. As a result, gallery owners and collectors seized existing copies and placed large, last-minute orders with the photographer. The gamble was that Adams would one day be in popular demand. The risk paid off.

There are approximately 850 prints of *Moonrise* in circulation. Museums account for perhaps sixty to one hundred *Moonrise* reproductions. When Gerald Ford was president, one adorned the White House. The largest known *Moonrise* is a thirty-seven by forty-five inch panel owned by a Los Angeles insurance company. By 1976, a standard sixteen-by-twenty inch *Moonrise* was going for $1,000. A year later it was up to $3,000. Twelve months after that, $5,000. When the Museum of Modern Art decided to hold a retrospective of Ansel Adams landscapes, the exhibit drove cost of a *Moonrise* through the roof. Christie's of New York recently auctioned off a twenty-one by twenty-six inch *Moonrise* for $12,000. Sotheby-Parke Bernet Gallery auctioned a similar size print for $22,000. A private sale of a single *Moonrise* reportedly netted $50,000.

Ansel Adams has never been back to Hernandez. "You don't return to a place to take pictures unless it's on an assignment," he says. Accumulated debris in the village aside, the original setting of Moonrise hasn't changed that much. The Catholic church in the left hand side of the photograph still stands. San José del Chama it is, chartered by the Mexican government in 1835. In 1945, the priest was Joseph Pajot, a Frenchman. Pajot died in 1947, and he was replaced by Walter Cassidy, who served Hernandez fourteen years. Cassidy was largely responsible for restoring the mission. In *Moonrise,* the church has a flat roof. It's peaked now, and made out of tin. Only during Holy Week are services held inside. A second church was completed in 1972, on the other side of the highway. It's also San José Church, but more often called in Hernandez the "new church." The new church would probably never find its way into an Ansel Adams photograph: it's a low-slung structure, made mostly of steel. "I go there, but I don't like the new church," admits Annie Borrego. "It reminds me of a warehouse."

The cemetery whose crosses glow in *Moonrise* still exists, though nobody has been buried there in years. Hernandez's deceased are now laid to rest behind the new church in, appropriately, the "new cemetery." And the little adobe house to the right of the church also survives; a kitchen and porch have been added to the home that was built in

1928 by Luis Roybal, Annie Borrego's father. Roybal died in 1978. Pausing by the door of "Reggie's," Annie Borrego asks, "Millions of people have seen my father's house, haven't they?" Assured that they have brings a smile to her face. "I'm glad," she says. "But do you know something? My father probably never even saw that picture."

For Sale

PEP—To anybody who has ever lived in a small town, the gags are always the same: that if you blink, you'll miss it; that it's so quiet you can hear the grass grow; that it's so small the zip code has only four digits. While Pep's zip code has the required numbers, if you want to talk small towns, you've come to the right place. Located in Roosevelt County, twenty-four miles south of Portales, Pep, not counting a dog named Trixie and a cat called Tom, has a population of two.

In recent years, a good many wide spots in the road that pass themselves off as villages have dried up. Rather than blow away completely, some of these towns such as Pep—small pieces of real estate which once played a vital role in rural America—are now actually up for sale.

"I'll take $28,000 for it—lock, stock, and barrel," says N. C. Cathey, one of Pep's two citizens. Cathey's wife, Jessie May, is the other Pepite. The $28,000 that Cathey is asking, brings quite a bit. The price tag includes a grocery store with post office attached, two gasoline pumps, a three-bedroom house, a well-house, a two-car garage, a feed shed, and one acre of land. "I got a 500-gallon propane tank out back," says N. C. "I'll throw that in for nothing."

The Catheys have resided in Pep for twenty-five of their sixty-eight years. N. C. has run the grocery and manned the gas pumps all that time. Until last year Jessie May was the postmaster. Now the Catheys want to leave. They say they want to live in a bigger city, like Portales, New Mexico, where one of their children has a home. The Catheys' health is good—"I've only had one set of false teeth," cracks N. C.—it's just that they want something else from their golden years. "I want to do some fishing," says N. C. The couple has advertised the town and has had a few inquiries, but nothing solid. "It would have to be somebody who doesn't want to live in a real big place," says N. C., with usual understatement. "Somebody who wants to get away from things."

The only thing that moves fast in Pep is the traffic on State Highway 18, which bisects the town. Oil trucks and big rigs barrel by at great rates of speed on this stretch of the Llano Estacado. A few stop at the Catheys's store or fill up at the pumps, but most high-ball on through without noticing Pep. Those who do drop in are mostly people from surrounding New Mexico farm communities that straddle the Texas border—tiny hamlets like Lingo, Causey, and Garrison. "We never heard of this place before we bought it," says N. C., taking a seat on a bench on the grocery's front stoop. "We were farming up in Texline, but didn't want to do any more when we saw this place for sale. We paid $18,000 for it back then, in fifty-three. Hasn't really gone up all that much. Why, the wife's sister just sold a house in Houston for $45,000 and it wasn't half as good as the one we got here."

The Catheys bought Pep from an E. V. Talley, who had

run the town for eight years. The origin of the community remains unclear. N. C. says Pep was founded in 1928 when a man named Ennis Cox moved the present grocery store from the town of Richland, New Mexico. Seven years later the Richland post office was moved to Pep. Not surprisingly, there is very little left of Richland. Some state historians claim Pep was named for the breakfast cereal of the same name. The Catheys don't buy that. Says N. C.: "Way I heard it was that when Mr. Cox moved the store here, a Mr. Hightower owned the water and a Mr. Bates, the land. Each feared hurting the other's feelings by naming the town after himself. That's when Mr. Cox looked out at Highway 18, which even then was a graded road, and predicted it would one day be busy, you know, peppy."

According to N. C., Pep was a lively place years back. "They tell me people would line their wagons up for miles to bring in cream and eggs. There was a ballpark across the road." Once there was even another store in Pep, around the corner. N. C. says he heard that in Depression days Pep used to have a family on about every half section of land.

The Catheys believe there needs to be a store in Pep. The nearest store is in Milnesand, New Mexico, thirteen miles south. Dora, seven miles north, has only a filling station. Business is slow in Pep, but it's steady. Occasionally someone drops into town unexpectedly. An airplane once landed on the pavement across from the grocery, and a glider, from a Hobbs air show, touched down near the well shed. "Used to be people would drop drunks off late at night right out in front of here," says N. C. "One night a woman stopped up to the home." "She said she was lost," interrupts Jessie May. N. C. shakes his head: "She was drunk."

Thanks to the Catheys, Pep is a cheerful spot. N. C.,

with his wide, open face, is the kind of man who tends to tell jokes like "What do you think Pep spells backwards?" Jessie May mostly smiles a lot. The Catheys don't make a big deal of it, but they won't turn anybody down for gas or groceries, no matter the hour. The weather's good in Pep, too. "There are lots of pretty days here," says N. C. "It gets dusty and windy but every place has its drawbacks." And crime, say the Catheys, is just about nonexistent in Pep. "Couple of fellers broke into the store once and took the cash register out back and pried it open," recalls N. C. "I was told the sheriff didn't catch up with them boys till they got to Turkey, Texas."

There's a post office in Pep because people—seventeen in all—live outside the town in, well, the Pep suburbs. When Jessie May ran the post office she worked from 8:00 A.M. to noon. "At Christmastime," she says, "I was really busy." Buna Cathey, Jessie May's daughter-in-law, is now chief mail sorter. Being a hopeful name, Pep draws widespread interest. The Funk Seed Company once sent the Catheys 500 postpaid envelopes of seed, asking the couple to please mail them. Collectors often write for the town's postmark. "And we're always getting mail meant for people in Pep, Texas," says Jessie May. Ironically, seventy miles east is *another* Pep. "It's a much bigger place," explains N. C. "It's got three or four businesses."

Business in Pep, New Mexico may be slow, but N. C. will be the first to tell you that jazzing up the inside of the grocery won't make things move faster. Men's dress shoes for sale, at least twenty years old, still sit in their original boxes. There are ten-year-old cans of air freshener, and knee pads for picking cotton. At the rear of the grocery, a large walk-in freezer serves as a coat closet. At the bottom of one shelf on a side wall sit a stack of marked down seventy-eight rpm records with more scratches than grooves.

"A lot of this stuff I bought in garage sales," says N. C. And then he adds the obvious: "A lot of this stuff was here when we came." The lost-in-time look of Pep is everywhere: a light switch promotes "Cavalier" cigarettes; to the right of the front door rests a 1959 calendar; a Model-T valve lifter stands in a corner.

Like many small towns, Pep is the kind of place where cash is unimportant; almost all the Cathey business is on credit. Yet out of the proceeds from the store and gasoline sales the couple has managed to build up a little nest egg. They say anybody who wants to could do the same. In a hushed voice, N. C. tells how that nest egg could get even bigger. It is not meant as a sales pitch, he says, just offhand information he'd like to share. "Some time back an oil company drilled a well two hundred yards north of here, but they didn't find anything. There is gas and oil all around here, though; that old boy who did the exploring work, he told me there's oil right under this here house and grocery. He told me Pep was sitting right on top of a big pool."

A retired Albuquerque man was the eventual buyer of Pep. Gray Alan Wilson, sixty-five, moved there with his wife, daughter, and grandson. Wilson got the community for $25,000. "It's one of those things you always dream about," he told me.

Remembering Reagan

GALLUP—Long before he promoted Boraxo, even before Bonzo was born, Ronald Reagan made a movie in New Mexico. It's not the old oater *Santa Fe Trail*. That one was made everywhere; Reagan's New Mexican opus bears a more distinctive name—it's called *The Bad Man*. As horse operas go, it's a one-note nag.

The time was 1940. As the United States was inching toward war, Hollywood was spewing out movies like rounds of mortar fire. It was a boom period: *Citizen Kane, The Maltese Falcon, Suspicion,* and *Sergeant York* were all made that year. A handsome, young gent with a ready grin was grinding out his share of films. Ronald Reagan had come to Hollywood only three years before but already had made a string of movies, some good, some bad. Earlier in 1940 Reagan made a good one: *Knute Rockne, All American*. Later that year, around Thanksgiving-time in fact, Reagan would ride into Gallup and put the trimmings on a turkey.

For years Gallup was known more for turquoise jewelry than celluloid. In the late 1930s, a West Coast entrepreneur named Joe Massaglia changed all that. Massaglia built a fancy Gallup hostelry and dubbed it the El Rancho Hotel. A gaudy, ornate monument to a once-glamorous era, the place still stands.

As Massaglia had hoped, the hotel proved attractive to Hollywood producers, and once there they discovered that Gallup was a good place to crank out grade-B Westerns. The sanguine-colored mesas outside town provided a spectacular backdrop. Through the 1940s, fifties and even sixties, scores of shoot-'em-ups were filmed around Gallup. By the mid-1960s though, the El Rancho had begun to fade. When it did, so did the trend toward making movies in Gallup. There was another reason for Hollywood's departure. Scenes around Gallup were getting too familiar. As one film buff put it, "How many times can you see the same canyon?"

If Gallup movie-making had an end, it also had a beginning: 1940 and the filming of *The Bad Man*. Lest some waggish Democrat seize an irony between the film's name and the future of one of its stars, let it be said that the "bad man" of the movie was not Ronald Reagan but Wallace Beery. Originally, *The Bad Man* was a three-act play written by a New Englander named Porter Emerson Browne. The play opened in New York City in 1920, was generally well-received by the critics, and ran nine months. The plot centers on a virtuous young man named Gilbert Jones (Reagan). Just returned home from World War One, Jones finds his "hard by the Rio Grande" ranch about to be foreclosed by a particularly nasty sheriff. Jones fights the eviction aided by his crochety Uncle Henry. His old friend Pancho Lopez, a bandido in the mold of Pancho Villa, also lends support. At story's conclusion, Lopez gives a glad-to-be-of-service *adios* to Jones: the young rancher has regained his spread as well as his long-lost girlfriend, Lucia Pell.

Always on the lookout for decent if unimaginative yarns, Hollywood drained *The Bad Man* in typical derivative fashion. A silent film was produced in 1923. Seven years later came a talkie. Ten years after that still another version went before the cameras, in Gallup. The studio behind the third go-round of *The Bad Man* was Metro-Goldwyn-Mayer. If one wonders why an outfit like M-G-M would sink money into such a tired number, the answer lies in casting. The movie would be a vehicle for Wallace Beery, playing Pancho Lopez. Beery, the onetime elephant trainer, represented enormous box office power. Even though he had played Pancho Villa in a film only a few years before, there was a great demand for Beery's big, gruff, soft-hearted presence.

M-G-M was also able to land Lionel Barrymore, as Uncle Henry. In the twilight of his career, the wheelchair-bound Barrymore was nonetheless a drawing card. Two fairly new talents—Ronald Reagan and Laraine Day—would portray the star-crossed youngsters, Gil Jones and Lucia Pell. Rounding out the credits was a competent group of character actors: Chill Wills, Henry Travers, Chrispin Martin, and Tom Conway. With an ensemble like that, and with the bankroll it must have taken to sign them, M-G-M probably regarded script quality as secondary. The film would be directed by journeyman Richard Thorpe.

Eighty-five cast and crew members arrived by train in Gallup November 17, a shivery Sunday afternoon. More than 1,000 persons were on hand to greet the company. The movie seemed doomed from the start. Gallup has been known to have nasty winter weather, and that November rain and snow pelted incessantly. Eventually, half the crew had to be sent home to Hollywood. They returned in early December for more shooting—and more lousy weather.

Despite the interruptions, *The Bad Man* was released on

March 21, 1941. The notices were not at all favorable. The *New York Times* said, "This is one of the most loquacious Westerns we've encountered in a long time." The *Albuquerque Journal* began its critique with a line of Lionel Barrymore dialogue: "This is the gol-durndest craziest piece of nothing I ever seen." As for Ronald Reagan, the *Times* called him an "ineffectual hero." Only the *Albuquerque Journal* was kind: "Reagan comes back near the good work he did in *Knute Rockne*."

If there was ever a movie more likely to be lost in silver screen limbo, it is *The Bad Man*. Only seventy minutes long, it rarely appears on television. If it weren't for Ronald Reagan, *The Bad Man* might be worth forgetting altogether. In his 1965 autobiography, Reagan gives the film two short paragraphs, both tinged with sarcasm. He recalls playing a "bankrupt rancher in seventy-five dollar jeans." Also remembered is a battle for camera angles with veteran scene-stealer Wallace Beery and a horse. "I came in third," says Reagan.

Though not exactly a household name when he arrived in Gallup, Ronald Reagan, oozing heartland American charm, left behind an admirable impression. "Reagan never turns down an autograph," the *Gallup Independent* noted. When some barefoot Indian children showed up on the set one day, the local newspaper cheered Reagan for organizing a fund that would buy shoes for the kids. Once Reagan and a handful of cast members visited the Gallup Rotary Club. Chill Wills, ever the jokester, introduced Reagan as "Mr. Jane Wyman." Reagan recovered to tell an embarrassing story on himself, now repeated often. As a young radio announcer he used to "broadcast" Chicago Cub baseball games from Iowa by using a Western Union wire service machine. When the machine broke down one day, Reagan had to stall for nearly ten minutes. The Rotarians lapped it up.

Before he left Gallup, Reagan told a reporter: "We like coming here because we find out what real folks make up the average community, and they discover that people in the films are just ordinary folks, too." A "native son" the Gallup newspaper called him. "He has made a large circle of friends here."

Time has reduced that circle to a small yet still enthusiastic group. Potsy Cresto has lived in Gallup sixty-nine of his seventy-one years. For most of his life Cresto owned and operated a trucking firm and bus line. Through the 1940s, Cresto hired himself out to film companies that came to Gallup. He scouted locations, furnished vehicles, and enlisted extras. In search of realism for *The Bad Man,* Cresto recalls going east of Gallup to Red Rocks State Park. "I looked for water holes, and places where no telephone lines showed." Eventually, Cresto helped steer M-G-M to Manuelito, a tiny settlement on the Rio Puerco, sixteen miles southwest of Gallup. There, an elaborate set, including a hacienda, barn, corral, and bridge was constructed. And there Cresto met Ronald Reagan. "One of the nicest guys I ever talked to. He was an A-One man. I've never seen anybody friendlier. His movie? Let's see. Lots of action, I think."

Leone Rollie has made Gallup her home since 1933. One evening in late November 1940, Mrs. Rollie and her husband went to dine at the El Rancho Hotel. Sitting in the lobby to greet them was a pleasant-looking man with a wavy pompadour. "He was very gracious, and so young (Reagan was twenty-nine.). You must remember that he wasn't very famous then. He was happy to meet me, though. Yes, I think I saw his movie. No, I don't remember much about it."

There is perhaps no one living in Gallup who was closer to *The Bad Man* and its now celebrated co-star than Herbert Stacher. Almost eighty, Stacher is retired from the coal business. For much of his life his hobby was motion picture photography. "I used to take my own sixteen millimeter home movies. When that moving picture company came to town I went out one day and asked an assistant director if I could take a few shots. He said okay, but told me to stay out of the way."

It was during a break in the filming that Stacher says he got acquainted with Reagan. "I asked him if I could take some movies of him. He said, 'What do you want me to do?' I said, 'Just walk toward me.' So that's what he did and that's how I got him in my movie." When lunch was served to the cast that day, Reagan jumped up on a flatbed truck and invited the young coal merchant to join him. "I told him, 'No, thanks'," says Stacher. "But he insisted. He asked the caterer to get another box lunch, then handed it to me. I always liked Ronald Reagan after that. Course I voted for him; whaddya think?"

The Bad Man opened in Gallup at the El Morro Theater, just down U.S. 66 from the El Rancho. Before the film came on each night, Stacher treated the audience to his home movie of the feature presentation. Because Stacher's show was without sound, a local radio station announcer agreed to provide commentary. ("And here's Ronald Reagan walking toward the camera. . . .") The memory of it all is clear to Stacher. "My little program," he says, "went over really good. Maybe better than the main show."

Good Ol' Boy

STANLEY—Iris Fisher speaks with a wonderful Welsh accent. "Everybody is always asking me where I come from," says this housewife who lives here. "When I told this to Bruce, he told me to just say 'Stanley.' He said no need to say anything else." Over the past few years, Stanley has learned to wear the fame that it didn't ask for as naturally as its favorite son wears a cowboy hat. Most of the 200 or so persons from around here are genuinely proud of two-term governor Bruce King, even though King's twangy accent is, to put it politely, less than mellifluous. Some folks here even laugh at the suggestion that New Mexico has three languages: English, Spanish, and Bruce King.

"Bruce was always a kind of leader," Joe Landon was saying the other morning. Landon, eighty-two, runs the only commercial enterprise in this ranching outpost eleven miles north of Moriarty. Landon's combination gas station and dry goods store has been a Stanley crackerbarrel fixture since the mid-1930s. On any given morning, most of Stanley is bound to come to Joe Landon's to buy bread, drink from the communal coffee pot, play dominoes, and maybe chat with Bruce. King lives a mile and a half away in an imposing red-roofed, stucco home. He stops by Landon's store three to four times a week—unless he's out politicking.

"The Kings?" says Landon, adjusting his glasses. "Gosh, I guess I've known them since Bruce's daddy homesteaded here way back. Now they got ranches everywhere. I doubt they know how much land they got. Every hill out there has a King home on it. I don't know what they're going to do when they run out of hills." Indeed, a local telephone directory lists ten Kings in Stanley. In addition to Bruce and his wife Alice's spread, Sam and Don King (Bruce's older and younger brothers) have places nearby, as does King's sister, Leota, and her husband. Then there are the ranches of *their* children. The King Brothers Ranch—which is actually several ranches in several counties—has 15,000 head of cattle, plus alfalfa that stretches beyond the horizon. It is one of the biggest farming-ranching operations in New Mexico.

"A lot of people think Bruce accumulated all his money through politics," says Everett Dennisson, another old-timer. "That's just not true. Bruce and them other boys made their money through ranching. Even now Bruce don't hesitate to go out and do a day's work. He's not lazy, and they're all like that." The King boys got that way, believes Dennisson, from their parents, William S. "Bill" King and his wife, Molly. The couple arrived in Stanley from southwest Texas in 1919. Like many homesteaders of that era, the Kings plunked down their life savings on 160 acres and dreamed of making it as bean farmers. Several droughts during the twenties and thirties sent Stanley homesteaders back home. The Kings stayed; they toughed it out. Eventually they bought out their neighbors. By 1949, the year of Bill King's death, the family's Stanley

tracts had grown to more than 20,000 acres. Now an energetic eighty, Molly King still resides on the original homestead.
Ironically, as the King holdings grew, Stanley shrunk. At one time the town was a thriving city. It had two of everything: two hotels, two restaurants, two blacksmith shops, two copper mines. For a week it had one saloon— until the community closed it down. Save for a few dozen homes and Landon's store, all clustered about a single crossroads, there is nothing left. In fact, downtown Stanley has become almost a ghost town. Abandoned buildings are everywhere. The Stanley Public School, once a lively, yellow, concrete structure, built in 1936, is now a crumbling, deserted monolith. Windowless, its great walls are covered with graffiti. "When the school graduated its last class in 1962, it was a sad day," says Iris Fisher. "A lot of life just seemed to pass away. Stanley School, you see, was the social center of the town." In its glory years, the school had about 300 students in twelve grades. Bruce King, the school's most noted graduate, received his diploma in 1942.
"It makes me sick to go near that school now," says Everett Dennisson, who janitored there for forty years. "I helped to build it. It was one of the last WPA projects. Now, nobody cares." Rumors concerning the school building's future surface constantly. Someone wants to convert it to a private residence. Someone wants to turn it into a home for troubled teen-agers. There's talk of a trailer factory moving in; a windmill manufacturing plant.
If Bruce King is remembered for anything at Stanley School it is his football prowess. "Old Bruce," says Dennisson, "he was a big boy even then, like his daddy. Bruce played guard or tackle. He weren't rough. In a game, he'd pick up boys and drop them on the ground gentlelike instead of slamming them down. But if a boy on the other

team was a dirty player, look out. More than once I remember Bruce shoving a player's face in the ground."

Even in decline Stanley has a way of never letting go of its own. Each October the town holds a homecoming reunion for former residents. This year nearly 200 came from both coasts of the United States. For those who live here permanently, the attachment seems intrinsic. Jack Smith is Everett Dennisson's son-in-law. Each day Smith commutes 110 miles roundtrip to Albuquerque to work. Smith wouldn't have it any other way. "I don't have to listen to sirens or horns all night," he says. "And way out here I can whup my wife and nobody can hear her scream." Smith turns serious when Bruce King's name is mentioned. "When my house burned down, Bruce was there to try to put it out. Right there he wrote me out a check for $200."

Womenfolk in Stanley think so much of King that he is invited to speak to the Homemakers Club nearly every month. And just as regularly King attends services of the nondenominational Stanley Union Church, the community's only house of worship. During his first term as governor, King several times summoned the entire town to the governor's mansion in Santa Fe, forty miles away. "One year he threw us a really lovely Christmas party up there," says Iris Fisher, who has lived here since World War II when she met her rancher-husband Leroy in her native England. "Success has never gone to Bruce's head. He remembers us."

Few will deny that Stanley is dependent on King. The King Brothers Ranch employs about thirty-five persons. During harvest time, the figure is close to one hundred. "I know I'm prejudiced," says Jack Smith, "but Bruce is a good ol' boy. Like all politicians, I suppose, some people like him and some don't." The last time he ran for election, out of 146 votes cast for governor in Stanley precinct, 124 people liked Bruce King.

You could laugh about Bruce King's way of talking, but you have to admire his fairness: after this story appeared, Governor King never so much as offered me a job—not even one shovelling manure.

5: Givers

"I guess I'm somebody they can look up to."

The Champ

LORDSBURG—The plot reads like a Hollywood script: *Young, teen-aged punk from broken home, in trouble up to his incorrigible ears, is sent off to live with tough but tender uncle . . . there discovers world of boxing.* If this was a B-movie, our hero would probably be punching his way to fame. The problem, and it's only a problem if you want no part of realism, is that what the kid gains from boxing, as well as from his uncle, he turns around and gives right back.

The barrios of San Bernardino, California have long been mired in street gangs. When Ruben Gomez arrived there from Lordsburg with his family, he was six-years-old, one of ten children. By the time he was thirteen, Ruben never went anywhere in San Bernardino without taking a baseball bat—for protection in his acts of delinquency. He began with bicycle thefts then, his courage heightened by daily whiffs of clear enamel, with break-ins at furniture stores and the corner grocery. One night Ruben and his gang decided to knock over a private residence. The home had a burglar alarm and police arrested Ruben and several others. More arrests followed. After

Ruben was nabbed jimmying the back door of a convenience store, his mother sent him back to Lordsburg to live with an uncle, Oscar Gutierrez.

"I was real scared," says Ruben who up until that time had never been afraid of anything. "I could remember my Uncle Oscar from when I was a boy; how he once made me apologize to a man whose son I picked on." Oscar and Irene Gutierrez had no children of their own when Ruben arrived. What they did have was a great deal of patience and understanding. In California, Ruben had been used to coming and going as he wished. A chip on his shoulder had grown to Sequoia size. Oscar laid down the law: Ruben would go by Oscar's rules or he wouldn't go at all. Up at dawn every day, Ruben would accompany his uncle on the older man's milk route. After work, Ruben would work on the home Oscar was building. That fall, Oscar walked his nephew down to school to enroll him personally.

"In California," says Ruben, "I though I'd never finish school. In New Mexico, I actually found I liked it." The schoolwork was hard, but with the Gutierrezes encouraging him, Ruben kept up. The gang life he had once known was traded for after-school sports. In high school he earned state honors in football and baseball. Toward the end of his final year at Lordsburg High, Ruben and his class went to Phoenix for their senior trip. There Ruben saw a movie that would change his life—*Rocky*.

Upon returning to Lordsburg Ruben got out a duffel bag, filled it with rags, and hung it from a tree in his girlfriend Lisa Talavera's backyard. A punching bag was born. Soon Ruben searched for a better training site. Lordsburg had a modest youth center, but no real place where a youngster could let off steam. Lordsburg had never been a boxing hotbed: a fight in town used to mean two people would be going out into the desert to square off. Ruben kept searching. Adjoining the rear of the Black Cat Lounge was a deteriorating, abandoned building. Built in the early 1930s, the structure had been a casino, dance hall, bar, and most recently, the Elks Club. When Ruben poked his head in the door and looked beyond the half-inch layer of dust and past the crumbling ceiling, he saw the building's future—a boxing club.

Cleaning the place was a heavyweight task. Floors and walls had to be completely remodeled. Paint was needed inside and out. Ruben did most of the work himself. "I wanted to quit," he says. "I would be nailing by myself at night and I'd think, 'what for?'" But Ruben knew why he couldn't stop: the boxing club would not be for himself but for the street kids of Lordsburg.

To make it truly a community project, Ruben held a taco sale. From the proceeds he bought equipment. Then he held a second taco sale and a third. But even in heavily Hispanic Lordsburg, one can hold only so many taco sales. That's when Ruben decided to go to the mayor. Marching into a city council meeting with twenty-five youngsters behind him, Ruben pleaded his cause. Touched, Lordsburg purchased $350 worth of boxing supplies. The homemade duffel bag had seen its last days.

There remained, however, the matter of learning how to box. What Ruben knew about the sport he had picked up on the movie screen from Sylvester Stallone. Occasionally, an ex-bantamweight champion of Arizona would drop by the club to give pointers. But mostly Ruben learned—and taught—on his own. Tall, engaging Lisa Talavera was always there to help, though. When Ruben needed ring ropes, he got hold of some garden hose, wangled some bed sheets from Haskell's Linen Supply, and Lisa sewed the conglomeration together. From old pillows Lisa fashioned corner cushions. Still, Ruben wasn't satisfied. He took his story to a Hidalgo County commissioners meeting. Out of that visit came $2,100 worth of equipment, including ten pairs of gloves, mouthpieces, a doctor's scale, a bell, and a medicine ball. When the white-with-blue-trim doors of the Lordsburg Boxing Club opened, teams from Las Cruces, El Paso, and Tucson showed up for matches.

As the club developed, Ruben cut down on his own boxing. A middle weight, he has had five fights, winning three. "I started out too late," he says. "Besides, if I want to do this right, I need to devote myself to the kids. I counsel them, chauffeur them, train them, teach them what little I know." Then, sounding like any boxer who is supposed to be retired, "Still, if the right fight came along, well...."

Even though the club is a priority, Ruben cannot give it all his time. After he graduated from high school, Ruben took a job with his uncle and moved into a small home by himself. Slowly, siblings from California were sent to Lordsburg to live with him. For the last two years Ruben has worked the milk route, run the club, and single-handedly raised three younger brothers and a sister.

The hours he does give to the club are precious. Wiry mites like Raymond Perea at fifty-seven pounds, and Rudy Holguin at seventy, and Roy Atilano at eighty, seek Ruben's advice, lean on his every word, pull at his sleeves. Ruben knows the reason: "I guess I'm somebody they can look up to, somebody to give them, how do you say it?—confidence—like my Uncle Oscar did me." Ruben is especially happy about the confidence he's been able to give 115-pound Eddie Romero, a "natural" fighter. Ruben says Eddie reminds him of himself. "Eddie was a regular little hoodlum when he came in here. He was into drinking and stealing cars. I guess he took me as his big brother. A lot of the kids out there have talent, some like Eddie's. Many of them are throwing it down the drain."

At the core of everything Ruben does is Oscar Gutierrez. A stocky, temperate forty-two-year-old, Oscar says he spoke with Ruben's California probation officer before his nephew came to live in Lordsburg. The kid couldn't be handled, Oscar was told. Oscar likes challenges. "I'm really proud of Ruben," says Oscar who now has two small children of his own. "In California, he was confused—he never really knew his real father. Here in Lordsburg he's accomplished so much and all of it by himself. He's helped reduce the crime rate, I know that. You don't see many kids hanging around on street corners here anymore."

Some people feel Ruben has tried to mold himself into a carbon copy of Oscar. In high school Ruben wanted the same football jersey his uncle had worn. As great as the admiration has been, the two have had their differences, as anybody who works side by side will. For a time in high school, Ruben moved out of the Gutierrez's home. He wanted a car and Oscar said no. "Really, I was madly in love with Lisa," says Ruben. (The two are now married.) Ruben says his uncle occasionally "gets on my case," especially concerning the milk route, which Ruben will someday inherit, but Ruben knows he can never stay mad. Says Ruben simply: "Uncle Oscar, he made a man out of me."

The handsome, twenty-one-year-old man Ruben has grown into has not reached his goal. Standing in the way is a boxing club that has become cramped and in need of major repairs. A drafty, unheated building in winter, in the summer the club's air conditioning is an open door. "I don't like to put down this town," says Ruben. "They've helped me in so many ways. But I'm still all alone here. Parents should be coming up to me and saying, 'Here,

Ruben, here's a bigger and better building you can use.' I'm no glory hound. I just want others to be involved."

Whenever he thinks about the remaining work, how the roof might fall in any day, Ruben says he is reminded of *Rocky*, and an all-heart prize fighter who went the distance. Ruben knows what might have been—if he had quit. "One of the guys I used to run around with in California is in the pen for life. Another is an addict and dying. Another is brain-damaged from sniffing that enamel. I guess I was pretty lucky."

This story earned Ruben a spot in People *magazine. That didn't make him nearly as proud, he told me, as becoming a father—"of a little guy with a good jab."*

The Flight of 59816

LAS VEGAS—If the value of a human being cannot be computed in dollars and cents, what is the worth of those who work to keep someone alive? This is the story of three young people and their flight to save the life of a fourth.

It is 8:45 P.M., a Thursday. A Piper Navajo airplane has just left Albuquerque and is bound for Las Vegas. In that city lies a baby boy. Two hours earlier this infant had come into the world two months premature. His weight is just shy of three pounds. Of crucial concern, however, is something called RDS, a potentially severe respiratory disorder many premature babies encounter. This baby has RDS.

The airplane's pilot is employed by Southwest Air Rangers of Albuquerque. He has made this kind of run—retrieving babies born with defects and transporting them to Bernalillo County Medical Center's neonatal Intensive Care Unit—several times. A BCMC nurse aboard the plane is also experienced with these flights. A medical doctor on the plane is on his first trip.

The October night air has a snap to it. Inside the plane it is warm and getting warmer. There's a tension about, an anticipation that can only be felt when there's a life at stake. Ron Waterman, the pilot, checks with his radio. "This is Lifeguard Five-Nine-Eight-One-Six," he says. "Lifeguard" signifies any kind of medical mission—from kidney transplant to plague victim. Sometimes Waterman will say "Urgent Lifeguard." He has been flying since he was twenty-one. He is twenty-nine now and has 4,200 hours in the air. "Half a year," he says. A bachelor with a barnstormer's moustache, this evening Waterman was napping through a television show when Southwest Air Rangers called him for this emergency. He is wide awake now.

Seated beside the pilot is Dr. Christopher Merchant, twenty-eight. He was working in BCMC's newborn nursery when the flight alert came. Bespectacled and wearing a white golf cap, Merchant has the look of a quiet scholar. But Merchant is doing a lot of talking tonight—about baseball, fly-fishing, his job at BCMC where he is a second-year resident in family practice. He's talking a lot, he admits, because he's more than a little nervous this first time out. "I'm glad I volunteered, though," he says in a Virginia drawl. "The way I look at it, there are two kinds of doctors: those who can't get real near a sick patient and those who aren't disturbed by intensive care. I'd like to think I'm the second kind."

Seated behind Waterman and Merchant is Karen Zapalac, twenty-six. She is from Texas originally, and is a registered nurse. She estimates she has been on more than 100 ICU flights since coming to BCMC two years ago. Karen had just come in from jogging earlier tonight when the hospital called. Short, with close-cropped hair, she's dressed in Levi's and a denim jacket with flowered patches. The small plane sways. "I've never really been airsick," she says shyly while staring out the window. "Oh, last week we were coming back from a run to Gallup and my stomach felt funny. But you learn to handle it." Karen, like Chris Merchant, has already put in a full day's work in the hospital. As a single person, she could easily be doing something else tonight. "I probably go on these things more than anybody," she says. "I'm no goody two-shoes, though. Sometimes I hesitate when they call me, say yes, then wonder why I did."

Twenty minutes outside Las Vegas, Ron Waterman calls ahead for an ambulance. With luck, the vehicle will be at the airport when they arrive to take Karen and Chris and a portable isolette to Las Vegas Hospital. "In some places," says Karen, "there's only one ambulance service and if they're out on call the waiting around can get pretty frustrating." Because small hospitals often do not have on hand necessary stabilizing equipment for preemies, the BCMC transport team carries its own. And because Chris and Karen are experienced in working with preemies, they go to the hospital to work rather than meet the baby at the airport. "There's not much you can do once you're in the air," says Karen.

At 9:20 P.M. Lifeguard 59816 touches down at the small hilltop airport. Luck is running against the transport team; the ambulance hasn't arrived. Fifteen minutes later, Karen and Chris breathe concomitant sighs upon sighting a gold-colored van roaring across the macadam. Within three minutes, an isolette, a cardiac monitor, an I.V. pump, an emergency medical kit, a doctor and a nurse are aboard the ambulance and on their way.

Ron Waterman has elected to stay behind. Chris and Karen may be a long time at the hospital—sometimes it takes up to six hours. Waterman feels more at home in airports, anyway. Like most men accustomed to working nights, Waterman takes his coffee black. Sipping a cup, he says he came to Albuquerque only a few months before.

He arrived without a job and without knowing a soul. He had left San José, California, where he owned his own flight school. After selling the business he headed for a part of the country he had never seen—and a new challenge. By the first of May he had a job with Southwest Air Rangers. "Plenty challenging," he says. Waterman gets all sorts of flying assignments. "Bodies to bankers," he calls the work. The bodies are flown to BCMC for autopsy. Bankers are much better company. Waterman will often ferry them to Pagosa Springs, Colorado, for a weekend of condominium-inspecting. Yet for all the majestic mountain air, the golf, and the Jacuzzis Waterman samples at Pagosa, it's clear he enjoys ICU flights more. "This is just a special kind of service."

It became special the day Waterman went off to Roswell to bring back a baby who suffered brain damage during delivery. On that particular day Waterman decided to go to the hospital. In the lobby he met a young man who turned out to be the father of the infant the transport team was picking up. "He started asking me questions about what our service would cost," says Waterman. " 'I make $800 a month,' he said. 'I'll pay for it.' He was so broken up for his wife I thought he was going to cry. But he was so courageous and brave it was hard to look at these trips impersonally after that." Eventually, that Roswell baby was returned to its mother—the goal of all transport teams.

Shortly after 11:00 P.M. the ambulance returns from Las Vegas Hospital. The stabilization went well, reports Chris Merchant. "The doctor there had things all ready for us." Pulling the isolette aboard the plane, Chris and Karen look down at the tiny, sleeping baby, a baby without yet a name. Waterman takes a peek. "Cute little guy, isn't he?" the pilot asks. As the plane glides down the Las Vegas runway, a jackrabbit, not much bigger than Lifeguard's newest passenger, scurries out of the aircraft's path. At 11:16 P.M., 59816 is airborne. Scrunched behind the cockpit, Karen and Chris monitor the baby's condition. Heart rate, temperature, and respiration are recorded in a notebook. Reaching through a porthole in the heated isolette, Karen adds more warmth by stroking the infant with her bare hand. "Anytime you pick up a baby," Karen says, "you automatically feel close to it. And partly responsible for it." Karen remembers losing only one baby during an ICU flight. A year ago, a preemie with RDS ceased breathing as the plane landed in Albuquerque. Karen says her biggest concern is that the life-supporting equipment doesn't fail. If it does, Karen says she prays. A Catholic, she has, on occasion with parent's permission, used the droplets from a syringe to baptize a baby in flight. "I do it because I know what my feelings are. If the baby should take a turn for the worse, it's better this way."

Turning his head around in the pilot's seat for a moment, Ron Waterman watches the still figures behind him. One of the hardest things for a pilot to do, he says, is not to worry about the patient. At 11:43 P.M. Waterman radios ahead for a BCMC ambulance. Still breathing laboriously, the baby continues to sleep. Red and green lights from the plane's dashboard, and white lights from within the isolette, give the cabin the appearance of a Christmas tree.

When Waterman catches the glow of Albuquerque he begins his descent. It has been a cautious, rocky ride back. "When you're flying babies like this, ones that can't breathe well, you want to go to an altitude that won't put a lot of stress on their lungs," says Waterman. "Sometimes you sacrifice smoothness for a lower altitude."

The outline of a waiting ambulance is spotted as Lifeguard 59816 puts its wheels down. Personal belongings are quickly gathered. Chris Merchant fishes from beneath a seat a brown paper sack, unopened. "My lunch," he says, grinning. Merchant's nervousness has long since given way to a weary excitement. After delivering the baby to BCMC, he and Karen will return to the hospital for work at 7:00 A.M. Ron Waterman, too, will get little sleep this night. In three hours, his pocket beeper will go off again and he'll be on his way to Roswell—another sick baby.

Just before the plane's back doors swing open, the trio glances down once more at the miniature cargo that has occupied their evening. Wrapped in a spiderweb of tubes, and hanging onto life, the infant suddenly gives reason why these last four hours have been worth everyone's efforts. Wriggling his small head back and forth, the baby flashes his eyes—for the first time ever. They are blue. It is two minutes past midnight.

A Dad Named Eddie

SANTA FE—Out toward the south end of Cerrillos Road, in a crippled and undernourished trailer park, Eddie Staup stands on the doorstep of his white mobile home. Two small boys, not more than five or six years old, tug at his trouser leg. "Dad?" each asks. "Would you, Dad?" A baseball is held up. "Sure," says Staup, grabbing the ball and tossing it first to one boy, then the other. "Throw it to me, Dad," pleads a third boy, joining the first two. "Hey, Dad," calls a fourth, walking over. "When do we eat, Dad?"

Were Eddie Staup the kind of fellow given to philosophy, he might have coined, "If you have to beat a child, for God's sake use a string." A threadbare Father Flanagan, Staup looked around nearly half his life for something meaningful to do. Suddenly he realized he had been doing it for years—caring for hard-luck kids.

Most children are fortunate to know one father. Some know none. Then there are those kids—the abused and the rejected, mainly—who happen upon Eddie Staup. He may not be their father, but he is most certainly their Dad. By appearances, Eddie is not a usual Dad. A hook-nosed, stooped man of fifty-five, tattoos ornament his boney arms. Unfiltered cigarettes make unending trips to a mouth that, when open, shows more gum than teeth. Staup has never much cared much what adults think of him. His concern is for the little people of life. "Even when I was in junior high school," he says, "I liked to go out and watch the youngsters. I don't know what I got out of it all."

   The son of a barber, Staup was born in Nashville, Michigan. The hair-cutter urged his son to try everything in life until he found what he wanted. After Army service in New Guinea in World War II, Staup worked as a television repairman, racing car driver, garage mechanic, security guard, drive-in owner, and grocery store manager. It was while running the grocery in a tough, black section of Denver that Eddie's special relationship with kids began. "I was putting some cans on the shelf one day when a little seven-year-old came up to me and started helping. He asked if he could stay with me. I said sure, not really knowing what he meant. A half hour later, the boy came back with a red wagon filled with all his clothes. He really wanted to *live* with me."

   Eddie discovered the boy's mother was divorced and on welfare. She agreed to let Staup have her son. Not long after that Eddie took out a foster care license. He had to; there were now nine boys living with him. Eddie would keep the youngsters as long as he could, working to return them to their natural parents or providing interim care until a foster parent could be located.

   When homes were found for all the boys, Eddie decided to move on. He sold the grocery and came to New Mexico. In Albuquerque he bought a trailer and took a job as a security guard. Soon he became acquainted with four young brothers, children of abusive parents. For three years the quartet lived with Staup. He worked to build a better relationship with the boys and their parents. Eventually, the family moved to Santa Fe. Not knowing what else to do, Eddie followed. Taking a mobile home close to the brothers, Eddie let his magnetic forces go to work. He soon became known as a man who wouldn't turn down any child. "Eddie is one of the most dependable foster parents we have," says Rita Seeds of Santa Fe County's Department of Human Services. "In fact, I think we place too many kids with him. But Eddie just won't say no. He'd give up his own bed to help a kid."

Since Eddie's trailer also serves as a licensed day care center, there are few beds in sight. Eddie takes kids at any age. The Human Services Department brought him a one-year-old boy found wandering Santa Fe Plaza dressed in only diapers. He takes them at any hour. "We've called Eddie at three o'clock in the morning," says Rita Seeds. "He says, 'Bring 'em right over'." And he takes them with any problem. "I've seen some kids come here so beaten you wouldn't recognize them," sighs Eddie.

Once Eddie was given an eight-year-old named Deana. Deana had never spoken a word in her life. "I held out a cookie to her," Eddie says. "I kept doing this, holding out a cookie, then putting it back in my pocket, all the time saying 'Cookie'." The next time Eddie saw Deana was during a visit Deana made from her foster mother's home. Running toward Staup, arms outstretched, Deana threw herself onto Eddie. "Cookie!" she shouted.

There have been others. Juan, twelve, was an incorrigible with a penchant for swearing. "I let him know who was boss," remembers Eddie. "I've got a little bar of Lifebuoy in the bathroom." Ricky, six, had been sexually molested by both parents. "I just tried to give him a little something extra," says Eddie. "Tried to love him more." Troy was a ten-year-old glue sniffer who liked to break windows. "He wants to come live with me now full-time."

Instead of adopting children, Eddie's goal is to make

things easier for the child's real or foster parents. When Eddie agrees to take on a child, he will not allow the parent to call or visit for three weeks. This sometimes angers a parent, but Eddie refuses to alter his methods. "Once he has a boy for even a short while," says Rita Seeds, "the child seems to fit in better. Eddie has some kind of magic."

It doesn't take too long to locate the source of that wizardry. Two scrapbooks lie open in Eddie's wood-panelled living room. One book is filled with grisly newspaper articles on child abuse from around the country. "Parents Get Ninety-nine Years in Child's Death," reads one headline. "Judge finds Woman Guilty in Baby's Torture," says another. Alongside several articles Eddie has written "Why? Why?" A second scrapbook, a much happier one, has snapshots of many of the children Eddie has looked after over the years. There are photographs of kids swinging bats, throwing footballs, horsing around. At the front of this book is a special photograph. It is a picture of a blond-haired boy wearing an enormous smile. The boy is Lukie Staup. Fifteen years ago, Lukie, along with Eddie's wife, died in an automobile accident. Their car was struck by a drunken driver.

Eddie's eyes mist. "I still haven't been able to get over it. Lukie was eleven when he died. A good little ballplayer." Eddie admits much of what he does is because of Lukie. Lukie is Ricky and Deana and Troy and Juan and all the others. Simply, Lukie Staup is anybody in need of more than a father.

Not long ago, a small boy named Freddy, a neighborhood kid from a few trailers down, stopped Eddie on the street. "I sure wish you were my Dad," Freddy said. Eddie Staup, a man who knows a good home is hard to find, said, "I sure wish I was too."

A Real Gas Pain

HOBBS—Spiraling natural gas bills are like atmospheric conditions: each elicits complaints, but little action. One who has responded, though, is Reverend Frank Wells, who has been known to go after the Hobbs Gas Company with, if not the wrath of God, then a furious storm of indignation. "The Hobbs Gas Company," says Wells of its seemingly endless rate increases, "doesn't read meters; it reads the weather." Some people believe the only way that will ever change is if Frank Wells changes the weather. And there are a few who believe he could do just that.

Hefty home fuel bills around Hobbs are like the town's bubbly oil fonts—they come with the territory. Although it sits in the energy-rich Permian Basin, Hobbs has among the highest natural gas rates in New Mexico. No matter that the Hobbs Gas Company owns a firm that produces natural gas. Never mind that the Hobbs Gas Company owns another firm that transports natural gas. The rates still climb in part because the HGC uses intrastate gas that is not federally-controlled. The Reverend Frank Wells wants an explanation for the other part.

The Ebenezer Baptist Church is located in a mostly black section of Hobbs sometimes referred to as "The Flats." The church has no marker; people in The Flats know where the building is, as well as the whereabouts of their pastor, even when he's not in. "Reverend Wells likely be out stirring up a fuss," one congregant proudly informs a visitor. Like its preacher, Wells's church is all down-home theology. A sign over the pulpit advises, "Do Not Chew Gum in Service." Another sign in the vestibule is a cancelled check issued from "The Bank of Eternal Life, Powers Unlimited," and is made out to "Whosoever Believeth." Set off to the front of the church is a small ushers room. "That's where we hold our prayer meetings," says Wells, suddenly appearing. "We don't hold them in the sanctuary no more because our utility bills got too high." Wells is a short, jaunty man with the sausage-thick fingers of a day laborer.

Rocketing utility bills first came to Wells's attention about eight years ago. He was retired from the General Telephone Company after thirty years service. He had begun as a janitor there, rising, he says wryly, to "utilityman." Wells always held two jobs: the phone company and his church. He sits on many city committees, including the Cemetery Board. "Quiet work," he calls that. At seventy-two, he moves about in a peculiar, high-stepping stride a trackman might use to assault a hurdle. "The way I keep going," Wells explains, "is I keep going."

Eight years ago Wells decided never to stop going. Ebenezer Baptist parishoners had come to him with tears in their eyes and $100-a-month gas bills in their hands. These were families of The Flats who lived in two-room houses. To help what he has always called "God's little people," Wells formed the Concerned Citizens. Their target would be the Hobbs Gas Company.

The HGC was founded in 1929 and for many years was run by the Roy C. Marston family. In 1971, the company that supplies the gas needs of all Hobbs's residents and those in the surrounding region, was purchased by the late Jack F. Maddox. As Frank Wells had done, Maddox came to Hobbs from Texas in the 1930s. Maddox quickly built a reputation as a shrewd and influential businessman. He became president and chairman of the New Mexico Electric Service Company. For thirty-five years he was director of the New Mexico Bank and Trust Company. He sat on the boards of two colleges. He owned a pipeline outfit, an oil and gas development concern, and assorted real estate holdings. The story was that if Jack Maddox didn't own Hobbs, he surely was hunting its deed.

Power has a way of transmitting fear. While many in Hobbs respected Maddox, others were downright frightened of him. When the Maddox-run Hobbs Gas Company began seeking regular rate increases, few customers dared make waves. When the Hobbs Gas Company, with yearly revenues approaching four million dollars, said it needed the rate increases to attract long-term investors, the Reverend Frank Wells said enough was enough. Wells claimed the increases were helping to pay the utility company's dues at the local country club. A black man making such an assertion didn't endear himself to the all-white HGC nor did the lawsuit that followed, filed by Wells's Concerned Citizens. The suit took a while to get off the ground. When Wells looked for an attorney in Hobbs, a city that has more than fifty practicing lawyers, not one would take the case. No one wanted to face Jack Maddox. Wells was finally able to land the services of J. Lee Cathey—of Carlsbad.

Representing the Concerned Citizens has given Wells a second full-time job. When he appears before the state legislature or other governmental bodies, he often pays for the trips to Santa Fe himself. Other times he is given donations by Concerned Citizens, a few of whom Wells gleefully points out, are Hobbs Gas Company employees. "People are good about supporting things I start," says Wells. "I reckon if I started a fight, somebody would join in my side real quick."

That original lawsuit has caused Wells to make dozens of trips to the state capitol to testify, to intervene, and to attend Public Service Commission hearings. Once Wells made the 700-mile round-trip in a battered old Chevrolet in one day. Wells lives alone in a tiny bungalow near his church. He has outlived two wives, and his three children are grown. A Tide soap box overflows with legal briefs in his little front room. Ordained at fifteen, Wells has had scant formal education. Yet his vocabulary brims with terms such as "writ of prohibition," "petition for review," and "court injunction." Currently, the Concerned Citizens have four pieces of litigation pending.

• In the New Mexico Supreme Court, an appeal on the latest Hobbs Gas Company rate increases.

• In the U.S. District Court at Santa Fe, a suit to block the merger of the Gas Company, the New Mexico Electric Service Company, Minerals Incorporated (a Maddox-owned firm that produces natural gas for the two utilities), and Llano Incorporated (also Maddox-owned and an entity that delivers natural gas to the utilities.)

• With the Security and Exchange Commission in Washington, D.C., a protest filed to block the above merger.

• With the Public Service Commission in Santa Fe, a complaint filed that Llano Incorporated, through operation of a cryogenics plant, is removing butane from natural gas and thereby providing less heat for people's homes.

Like any activist, Wells knows the value of a public demonstration. Take the protest march he spearheaded in Hobbs in the spring of 1979. The march was to held on a weekday morning and nobody expected much of a turnout. But Wells is full of surprises. More than 300 persons followed him from city hall to the steps of the Hobbs Gas Company. Many more lined the sidewalks to watch appreciatively from a distance, fearful perhaps of the specter of Jack Maddox. Maddox died last year but his clout remains formidable in Hobbs.

Wells was in his glory that morning as he hurdled along, an unlikely hero wearing a big grin on his broad, brown moon-face. Arriving in front of the HGC, he shouted through a megaphone: "Who is more guilty? The man who pulls a gun or the man behind a desk with a pen? I say they're both guilty!"

The protesting hasn't accomplished all he'd hoped it would. He has not been able to halt, permanently, rate increases. But then, has anybody, anywhere? "What he *has* done," says Susan Williams, associate director of the Energy Consumers of New Mexico, a citizens' self-interest group, "is to confront things. He pursues ways to force change. He gives us all hope." "He's like the little Dutch boy and the dike," says Wells's attorney, Lee Cathey. "He's slowed down the flow of the water by putting his fingers here and there. In a monopolistic situation like they have in Hobbs, that's about all you can do."

There are those who tell Wells that his fight is useless, that gas companies have one of the strongest lobbies in New Mexico, that the Hobbs Gas Company is going to go right on asking for—and getting—rate increases. Frank Wells says that may be but he cannot foresake his "little people." Not now, anyway. "I own an automobile," he says, "but I don't own a garage. Why? Because when I drive in a garage I want to drive out the other side. I don't back out of nothing."

When Wells appeared in Albuquerque in 1981 to receive the Jefferson Award, a New Mexico community service honor, I asked him for an update. "Everything's moving," said the gas company foe, "toward the front burner."

Rescue in Rio Arriba County

DIXON—The landscape in this southeastern pocket of Rio Arriba County is rugged and hard. It is a terrain of washed out arroyos and blunt mesas, hills referred to by many as "mountains." The nearby Rio Embudo offers good fishing. But if you're hiking, locals caution there's no one around for miles should you get in trouble.

Intermittent rain fell on the area one Saturday in September 1980. During the late afternoon, in the remotest part of the region, a quiet, sloe-eyed thirteen-year-old named Michael Brown sat somewhat preoccupied before a little adobe house. The rain wasn't bothering Michael. What worried him was that he hadn't yet started supper for his father. Suddenly, the boy looked up to see a male hiker running down the hillside that leads from a nearby mesa. Strangers aren't common in this isolated wilderness, and the sight of the man, and his subsequent words, startled Michael. "There's been an accident!" the hiker shouted, out of breath. "Up on the mesa . . . Susan's hurt . . . real bad!" When the man asked if he could use a telephone,

Michael managed his first words: "We don't have one." Frantic, the hiker rushed off down a dirt road.

At about 6:30 P.M., Michael's father returned home and asked about dinner. Lem Brown shares the house with his son, and depends on Michael for a great many things. Some folks say Lem leans too much on the boy.

After telling his father about the hiker and the injured woman on the mountain, Michael then did something that for him took great courage. He told his father he couldn't get dinner. "I'm going up to look for that woman," Michael said. Shrugging his shoulders, Lem Brown went into the house in search of something to eat. Michael followed, and grabbed a flashlight, quilt, and backpack. Outside, he hopped on a battered Honda motorbike and took off up the hill for the mesa. After a mile or so the bike gave out and Michael set off on foot.

Though darkness was approaching, Michael pushed on. He was in a canyon he'd traversed many times. Though he did not know the woman's location, Michael did know her name. "Susan! Susan!" he called. Finally, a faint reply: "Help . . . help. . . ." Above him, crouched on a slab of stone protruding from the mesa, was a figure. Carefully, Michael inched his way up.

What he found on a tiny lip of rock, big enough for only one more person, was a terribly frightened-looking young woman dressed in jeans and a T-shirt. Immediately, Michael saw the seriousness of the woman's condition. Her right arm bore a nasty gash. Her left ankle was swollen and bones were poking out from the top of her tennis shoes. She was in shock. Tearing off his pack, Michael pulled out the quilt and wrapped it around the woman's shoulders. Unzipping his jacket, he took it and the backpack and made a pillow for her to lie against. In addition to taking a vicious fall, the woman had landed in a cactus patch.

A steady rain had begun, and with it came a penetrating chill. Grimacing, the woman revealed her name: Susan Peoples. "Who are you?" she asked. Michael told her he lived nearby, was a student at Española Junior High School. "I'm from Santa Fe," offered Susan, through chattering teeth.

The conversation continued like that: bits and pieces traded between two persons, one twice the age of the other, neither quite believing what was happening. "Where is the helicopter?" Susan asked after a while. "Why haven't they come yet?" Michael gently explained that a helicopter couldn't get into the canyon. "The rain won't let it," he said. Adjusting Susan's quilt, Michael added, "Everything's going to be all right."

Susan found that hard to believe, especially when she frequently felt herself slipping off the little ledge, which was about seventy-five feet above the ground. Each time Michael would grab her. As an hour, then two passed, Susan began to drift into semi-consciousness. To keep her awake, as he felt he must, Michael asked her about the accident.

Earlier that day, Susan said, she and her hiking companion, David Rand, had pitched a tent on the top of the mesa. Because of bad weather, they had spent most of the day in the tent reading. Just before suppertime, the rain let up. The pair had planned a spectacular meal: chicken teriyaki, wine from a cooler. They had even brought a cassette player to dine by. Before eating, they decided to go down a stream below the mesa to freshen up.

That done, rather than take an easy but more roundabout trail back to their campsite, Susan and David began to scale the face of the mesa. At first it did not seem difficult. Then it did. Rockslides abounded. Almost at once the face turned perpendicular. As Susan reached for a handhold halfway up, her grasp gave way and she fell—backward—off the mountain. Somersaulting, she bounced off one ledge, then landed feet first on another. The drop had been about thirty-five feet. When David realized Susan couldn't move, he went for help.

Scared out of her mind, wracked by pain, Susan now stared at that help—an apple-cheeked boy. This *boy* though, was holding up her right arm to stem the bleeding. And reassuring her that a rescue unit was on its way. This boy was something special, Susan thought.

Around 9:30 P.M., the two heard voices and spotted a flare. Michael yelled and waved his flashlight beam. In twenty minutes a small group had crossed the canyon and made its way near to the ledge. The arriving paramedics discovered it was not going to be simple taking Susan from her perch. A special rescue basket called a Stokes litter was required. Someone went to Taos to fetch one.

Communication between rescue workers was not simple either because walkie-talkies repeatedly failed inside the canyon. And an ambulance and four-wheel drive vehicles were hindered by the craggy countryside. During the agonizing wait, Michael continued to lend his services. He helped paramedics find and cut wood for splints. And he ran errands to a base that had been set up near his home.

It was nearly 1:00 A.M. when Susan was brought down off the mountain. She was taken first to Espanola Hospital, then to St. Vincent Hospital in Santa Fe. Later that day she underwent two and one half hours of surgery. A pin was inserted in her leg, and a hip cast applied. Tendons in her arm were sewn together. When a weary but exhilarated Michael Brown finally got to sleep, it was after 3:00 A.M.

The next time Susan saw Michael was three weeks later in Gov. Bruce King's office in the State Capitol. During a hurried ceremony, King presented Michael with a proclamation. Susan gave Michael a grateful kiss. "I couldn't believe how shy Michael was," Susan recalls. "He wasn't that way at all on the mountain. He really took charge up there." Michael was glad to see color had returned to Susan's face. "When we were up on the mountain, she was real, real pale."

Others at the governor's ceremony noticed that Michael and Susan actually resembled each other. Both are tall and slim, have fine brown hair, and are attractive in a boyish sort of way. They could, perhaps, pass for brother and sister. Additional similarities aren't as obvious. Susan and Michael come from broken homes. Susan's parents were divorced when she was four; Michael's mother died when he was small. His father has since remarried and divorced twice. More important is the way Susan and Michael were brought together. Before they went up on the mountain, each was searching for something. By the time they came down, they had found it.

Susan Peoples, twenty-eight, grew up in San Francisco. Five years ago, driving from California to Texas, she stopped in Santa Fe. Admiring the city, she stayed. Like a lot of young people who settle in Santa Fe, Susan embraced a laid-back if slightly rudderless lifestyle. She worked as a secretary, receptionist, restaurant manager, bookkeeper, house-sitter. She studied est, Transcendental Meditation, acupuncture. She was a free spirit, but not terribly happy.

Two weeks before her accident, Susan met David Rand, a thirty-four-year-old Santa Fe construction worker. A week later, the couple went on a hiking trip near Dixon. Susan remembers standing on a mesa and viewing a secluded little adobe, the house where Michael lives with his father. How romantic, Susan thought. She also remembers agreeing with David to return and camp the next week on the *other* mesa, the steeper one.

Just prior to that weekend, Susan had reflected on her rash of jobs and her various gurus. She knew she didn't have any direction; she felt she was running from something. Confined to a hospital for two weeks after her accident, and then homebound for months after that, she discovered what it was—herself. Most of her life, at least since her parents' divorce, Susan had closed herself off from others. "Nobody ever saw me cry," she says. "I'd never break down. I put up a facade. 'Everything's fine,' I'd say. But when it got down to real nitty-gritty things, I'd wall myself off, be real independent, a loner."

Susan believes the accident has worked to break down her wall. "I've come to see people care about me. I mean, friends were standing in line in the hospital waiting to see me, to help me, to do anything they could for me. It felt great." Susan says she also learned that crying, breaking down even, isn't wrong. One afternoon shortly after she got out of the hospital, it took her three and one half hours to mix a pound cake recipe. Several times during that ordeal she burst into tears. But again, "it felt great."

Previously, when something personal bothered Susan, her defense mechanism was to do something physical: go dancing for hours, run until dropping. In a wheelchair, then on crutches, and now on a cane, Susan finds she can no longer flee. "I've discovered the real me doesn't like running away. I don't want pity, but I do need people. I always have but never admitted it. If the accident taught me anything, it taught me how to accept love."

An eighth grade student, Michael Brown lists history and English as his two favorite subjects. "We're studying the War of 1812 right now," he says of the former. Of the latter, he reports, "I kinda like stories by Thurber." Math is not preferred. Science is "okay," especially when he gets to work on this year's project, a solar water heater.

Living where he does has formed something of a wall around Michael, too. Arthur Salazar, principal of Española Junior High, calls the youth a "loner." "We didn't know much about Michael till this happened," says Salazar. "He's a good kid, an average student; I know he's had it rough up where he lives."

Michael's home, the one Susan Peoples considered "romantic," is Spartan. Besides having no telephone, the place has no electricity or indoor plumbing. The house is two deserted miles from the school bus stop, the school is forty miles from there. Michael likes basketball, but transportation prevents him from doing anything after school except going home. And when he's home, Michael must, among many other chores, help his father run a small sawmill.

By all accounts, Lem Brown is a stubbornly individualistic man. College-educated, he prefers to eek out a living as a woodcutter. According to Michael, father and son have had their troubles living together. "But I know if I try hard to get along with him," says Michael, "it'll be something I'll appreciate when I get older." Lem Brown did not attend the governor's ceremony that honored his son's heroism. Michael, therefore, has been reluctant to speak about any adulation he's received, including a commendation letter from the president of the United States.

Nonetheless, what happened on that mesa has given Michael something he's never had and, say relatives, needed desperately—recognition. "It's given him tremendous self-respect and self-confidence," says Michael's ex-stepmother who lives in Dixon. "It was a very powerful experience, Michael's sorting it all out, but one thing is clear. He's changed since it happened. Changed for the better."

Susan says Michael's unexpected appearance and his comforting presence on the ledge, made her come to think of him as a "guardian angel." "Michael's a part of me," says Susan. "Hardly a day goes by when I don't think of him and what happened. I owe Michael so much. He caused a major turning point in my life." Hearing this makes Michael grow quiet. "If I had been where Susan was," he says, "I'd have wanted somebody to have helped me."

6: Overcomers

"Oh, my God. What have I gotten myself into?"

Eyewitness

ALBUQUERQUE—Patti Hopper is the mother of two small children. She is a polite, attractive woman married to an engineer. Patti's life had never been complex—and certainly never violent. Then one day in the fall of 1978 she happened to be in the wrong place at the wrong time. She witnessed a shooting, and reported it. Overnight, Patti Hopper's ordinary kind of life became complicated. What emerged, however, was an extraordinary kind of person.

September twenty-second was sunny and clear as Patti steered her family's station wagon past the La Llave Drug Treatment Center on Grand Avenue. Patti was car-pooling her three-year-old son, Ryan, and a neighbor's child to the preschool her church runs. Another child, Kristen Hopper, was in school.

Suddenly Patti heard a loud noise, like an auto backfiring. Turning her head, she says she saw in quick succession the following: first, a blur, like a body falling. Then—and this Patti says she saw clearly for several seconds—a man holding a gun.

Guiding her car into her church's parking lot, Patti

quickly turned off the engine. She told the two children to lie low while she nervously crept back toward La Llave. "I got as close as I dared and watched the man I'd seen drive off," she says. "I tried to get a license number, but I guess I was shaking too much."

Back at her church, Patti rushed inside and telephoned the emergency number of the Albuquerque Police Department. She carefully gave them all the details she could. By noon, Patti was back at her home in the Northeast Heights when Detective Steve Swanson of the APD telephoned and asked her to come downtown. For nearly two hours Swanson showed Patti police photographs of guns and automobiles. She also got some startling news: the shooting she had seen was a murder. The victim, Juan Rael, forty, had died shortly afterward of a bullet wound in the chest. "I thought *Oh, my God,*" says Patti. *"What have I gotten myself into?"* That would be a question many would ask Patti over the next several months.

Patti was back home at 4:00 P.M. when Swanson called again. A suspect had been picked up; would Patti mind looking at some mug shots? By this time, Patti's husband, Bob, had come home from work. Swanson arrived and spread several pictures across the Hoppers' living room coffee table. There was no deliberation; Patti immediately picked out the man she had seen that morning—a husky Hispanic with an Afro hairdo. To be certain, Patti asked if she could see the man in person. Swanson said he would see what he could do.

A long weekend followed. "I was practically sick to my stomach the whole two and a half days," Patti says. "Every time the phone rang my heart went *bump, bump.*" On the minds of Patti and her husband was the understandable dread of retribution. Was this the type of man who, upon discovering there was an eyewitness, might strike back?

On Monday morning, Swanson called Patti. A lineup had been arranged. Over the weekend, several of Patti's friends had told her if the police did set up a lineup, to not identify the suspect; to do so would only bring further aggravation.

The lineup room was pitch dark. A one-way mirror took up one wall. "The whole thing looked like something out of *Dragnet*," remembers Bob Hopper, who accompanied his wife. A few feet in front of the mirror stood five prisoners. Patti was given a pencil and a piece of paper with numbers one through five.

All five men fit her original description. "It was a real good lineup," Patti recalls. "Still, I saw my man right away." And just as she saw him the room became uncomfortable. Patti found herself ducking down, hiding her face from the one-way mirror. "I know it sounds ridiculous," she says, "but the man I saw do the shooting was staring right back at me."

A few days later Patti was asked to appear before a grand jury hearing. After five minutes of testimony she went home. Several days later Placido Perez, forty-two, the man Patti had identified in the lineup, was indicted for murder. He was freed on $200,000 bond.

As the months passed, Patti's anxiety grew. She had trouble sleeping. She wondered why, on the morning of the murder, she hadn't turned the corner a minute sooner or later. She also began to wonder whether she should have gotten involved. "Even after the lineup," Patti says, "people were telling me I should just forget the whole thing. 'Look at what it's cost you,' they said." There *were* monetary inconveniences. The Hoppers spent $120 on new deadbolt locks for their home. Because Patti feared driving the family car for several months afterward, an alternate means of transportation had to be acquired. Then there was the gas expense for the trips downtown, and the payments to baby-sitters.

What bothered Patti more than money was Placido Perez. "Placido," she began to call him, for she felt she knew him. Albuquerque police told Patti she was in no real danger. Perez would probably not retaliate against someone who was not part of the drug culture. That culture, Patti learned, has its own code. Those involved in drugs as heavily as Perez and Rael were, protect as well as get back at their own. Police also told Patti she was probably not the only witness to Juan Rael's murder. Steve Swanson estimated perhaps six persons were milling about that morning, waiting for methadone when the shooting occurred. None came forward.

More weeks passed. Just prior to Christmas Placido Perez was arrested for armed robbery in an Albuquerque supermarket holdup. He was jailed without bail and for the first time Patti Hopper felt truly safe. On January 16, 1979, Patti received a subpoena from the Bernalillo County district attorney's office to appear before a pretrial conference.

Handling the prosecution would be Chris Key, assistant district attorney. Key and Patti were joined at the conference by an attorney and a detective Perez's wife had hired. For an hour and a half they pecked away at her story—a standard approach to confuse an alleged eyewitness. Key worked to calm Patti, especially when Perez's attorney played the tape of Patti's original telephone call to police. On the phone Patti had said that man she'd seen had left driving a Riviera. That Perez owned a similar-looking Toronado became a major point to the attorney. Patti refused to change her story.

The Perez trial was delayed numerous times. Patti continued to hear from her friends. "Why not pull out?" one urged. Patti knew she couldn't. On April 10 she arranged for a baby-sitter and headed for District Court; the Perez trial was on.

When Patti entered the courtroom that afternoon she didn't believe what she saw. Placido Perez looked completely different. He had lost forty pounds. His Afro was gone, replaced by a slicked-back hairstyle. He had grown a moustache. "Placido had changed his appearance," says Patti, "but he couldn't fool me. He was the same person. I'd know him anywhere." Perez returned Patti's stare with a smirk. It was the same menacing look Patti swore he had given her months before in the police lineup room.

Patti was on the witness stand for two and a half hours. Perez's attorney hammered away at the "inconsistencies" in Patti's telephone call to police. Patti was obviously mistaken, he said: the defendant was not husky nor did he have curly hair.

Through it all Patti remained unflappable. It was only after she got home that night that she came apart. She had "blown the case," she cried to Bob. She had "not said the right things." Bob Hopper tried to comfort his wife. "I told her how proud I was of her, and I was. She was great. I don't think there was anything more she could have said in court." Though Patti was not to testify again, the pain and stress of the trial stayed with her. She asked for and received counseling from her minister, and tranquilizers from her doctor.

On April 19, Steve Swanson telephoned. "Did you hear the news?" he asked. "The jury found Perez guilty of first-degree murder." Patti dropped the phone. "I felt like a new person," she says. Bob Hopper was ecstatic. "I don't know what we would have done if they had to have a retrial. I think Patti might have had a nervous breakdown." On May 14, Placido Perez was given a life sentence.

"Patti made the case," says Chris Key. "She was one of the best witnesses I've ever seen—conscientious, careful, even when the defense played games with her. Yes, I'd have to say most citizens probably would have reported what Patti saw, but not if they knew what might follow. The thing about Patti was that she never, ever, considered what might follow."

"I've nothing but praise for Patti," says Steve Swanson. "Perez was a loser, but we never could get one conviction on him in nineteen years until now. He had so much confidence he could pull off a murder in broad daylight. Trouble is, he didn't know about Patti." Swanson adds that above all he admires Patti for what she received for her efforts. "Patti asked for nothing and that's just what she got." Actually, Patti did receive the normal fee for testifying in court up to six hours: eight dollars.

Bob Hopper says the attitude of some of their friends still hasn't changed much. "What gets me mad is that this was a killing so foreign to most people. Nobody really cares what happens to two heroin dealers and so nobody cares what Patti did."

Patti cares. She feels her faith in the police, the courts, and the justice system has been strengthened through the experience. "If all those people hadn't done their job," she says, "if they had somehow let Placido off, I don't know what I would believe in any more."

Wayne Wallace, Farmer

ESTANCIA—Dawn has not yet arrived in the Estancia Valley, but Wayne Wallace, farmer, has been up for nearly half an hour. A crewcut, rawboned man, Wallace is doing chores of a different sort. He is sitting at a large, round Formica table in his kitchen. In front of him is a cup of carbon-colored instant coffee, and a pad of yellow-lined note paper. Wallace says he gets up at this hour to "look things over." His wife, Barbara, explains it another way: "This is the time of day when we make it or go broke. This is the time of day when Wayne 'puts a pencil to it'."

Each year thousands of American farmers go broke. Wayne Wallace has come close on more than one occasion. That's why he rises early, writes down figures and formulas, and sees if he can grow enough food so that by selling it all at a good price he can buy enough back to feed his family.

Wayne Wallace didn't always have a sense of humus. The son of an Estancia Valley dairy man, Wallace left home at eighteen; he'd had just about enough of farming, especially milking. Thinking he might like ranch life better, Wallace went to Silver City to be a cowboy; however, it turned out that was not what he wanted, either. "Those old cowboys, they never got ahead," Wallace says, lighting one of the many cigarettes he smokes each day. Wallace knew he didn't want a "town" job. He wanted a "country" job. When he left Silver City in the early 1960s, with a wife and a small family, he found a gas station for sale. The station was back home, in little Estancia. It was a town job, but he took it anyway. A year or so later Wallace sold out and bought the farm he lives on today.

"It was tough at first, but I don't believe farming was as tough then as now." In the beginning, Wallace had eighty acres of corn and alfalfa. And while he once hated milking, in time he took in ninety dairy cows. In those days of the mid-1960s, Wallace farmed his land by himself and milked every cow twice a day. "It was too much work for one person, but not enough work to hire anybody."

A quiet, shy man, Wallace expresses himself best in one way: by doing relentless, grinding, muscle-wearying work. That is the way he built up his farm and by being a Thinking Man's farmer. When he sold the dairy cows in 1968, he labored hard to acquire 160 more acres of corn and alfalfa. In 1970, when a neighbor retired from the ranching business, Wallace leased 5,000 acres of ranchland from the man.

"People in town, they think we have a lot of money," Wallace says, pulling out another Camel. "They think I'm a land baron. They just don't know what it takes to be a farmer. They don't realize we got a gigantic mortgage here. They don't realize about the high price of fertilizer and diesel fuel increased. They don't realize about big stockpiles. Heck, this whole valley is stacked up with alfalfa."

Only in the last few years has Wallace had to put a pencil to it regularly. He doesn't mind, but being a Thinking Man's farmer *all* the time angers him after a while. "Things have become a kind of joke. We're working our tails off, but we're getting so many increases—steel, natural gas, electricity—that it becomes hard to find ways to make it. I could get priced out any day. We're getting so we're working our land different on account of energy costs."

Wallace mentions farm machinery as an example of how prices are climbing. In 1970, he bought a used tractor for $7,000. The same tractor today costs $30,000 new, $12,000 used. In 1973, Wallace purchased a hay bailer new for $2,900. Today one goes for $6,000. A repossessed corn chopper cost Wallace $5,000; a new one bears a $44,000 price tag.

To keep up with this inflation, Wallace thinks. But mostly he just works harder. "I like men who have come up from nothing. Men who had the guts to stick it out. Men who made it without inheriting it." That's the kind of farmer Wallace would like his sons to be. Bernie is seventeen, Donald, sixteen. Although neither knows for certain what he wants to be in life, neither wants to live in town. Town in this case is Albuquerque. "Oh, man," says Bernie. "All town is is cars and McDonald's."

Bernie and Donald do help out, but in the end it is their father who does most of the work. Last year he built by himself a 10,000-pound cattle scale platform. And almost single-handedly he put up a mammoth, heavy-duty, steel hay barn and machinery shed. "There's nothing Wayne can't do," says Barbara Wallace, a handsome, brown-haired woman. "If he loses the farm, I know he could make out. He's only forty. He doesn't like to think about going to work in town, but there are no fears with Wayne. That's why I married him."

Barbara Wallace works in town, at the Torrance County

assessor's office. She has the job because of what the Wallaces refer to as The Great Sheep Disaster. After putting a pencil to it, Wayne decided to buy 600 sheep. His pencil had a dull point; in a short time just about all the sheep died and the Wallaces were out $6,000. Working in town has not given Barbara any thoughts of leaving the country, however. "When I turn up the drive at night, it's like a great peace comes over me. Why, way out here we don't even have shades on the windows. You feel safe. When I go to town I'm always forgetting to pull the curtain in our motel room."

The business of farming being what it is these days, the Wallaces don't get a chance to stay in very many motels any more. They have cut out their yearly motor trip. They no longer buy snack foods of any kind. To tighten up further, Wallace continues to test, to experiment, to haul out his pencil. He bought the first bale accumulator in the Estancia Valley. He may install solar-powered water systems. Even remembering The Great Sheep Disaster he is toying with the possibility of raising and marketing catfish on the farm. When the telephone rings in the Wallace kitchen it is often a fellow farmer asking advice—where to get a sprinkler part, what type of motor oil to use, might Wayne like to lend out his hay grinder?

"Everyone has his own idea about how to keep a business in shape," says Wayne Wallace, farmer. He slips another Camel into the side of his mouth. "We got a big part of our life tied up in this thing, but each year it's getting harder to meet our obligations. Only way I find you can make a living in the country is to do the work of two men."

The Lodger

ALBUQUERQUE—It smells now, the house at Number 314. It smells the dank and musty smell, the stale-food-and-weary-people smell all old rooming houses seem to acquire. Wilfred Cobb's dingy front efficiency, which he shares with two Siamese cats, is part of that smell. Cobb's room is also part of a house that for many years breathed festive cheer. Someday it may again, though Cobb probably won't be there to see it. Number 314, with its smells and memories, has been sold. And Wilfred Cobb, with his two cats, has received an eviction notice.

Few Albuquerque families can boast of four generations who have lived under the same roof, who have owned the same home for eighty-seven years. For 314 Arno Street Southeast, those years are more than a piece of Albuquerque history; they represent the flow of life itself, including birth and marriage and death and, perhaps even rebirth. Number 314 sits on the east side of Arno, on the block between Silver and Lead. It's in the old Huning-Highland Addition, Albuquerque's first suburb. Many of the homes in the area, once sweeping in their Victorian grandeur, are now like 314—seedy and decaying. Some of the homes are being lovingly restored; the Department of the Interior has designated the neighborhood a historic district.

"This was a great old place," says Wilfred Cobb, standing on 314's sagging and paint-chipped front porch. "It's been good to me, but it'll all be over soon, I reckon." Number 314's exterior tan stucco is now discolored. Its shingles are tattered. Long gone are the large awnings that graced its three stories, and the splendid Virginia creeper in the front. "Lots of big shots used to visit here in the old days," says Cobb, who grew up some blocks away on West Gold Street. "Nobody much comes here anymore."

It was in 1885, sixteen years before Wilfred Cobb's birth, that Martin and Adelia Kellogg came to Albuquerque from upstate New York. A hard-working insurance man, Kellogg did well in the Southwest. By 1891, he ordered construction of a new home on Arno Street for his wife and four children. Kellogg's house would be first-class. The foundations would be of the best mortar. The walls of the highest-grade brick. Imported California redwood would be used for the fireplace mantels, for the door and window frames, for the stairway and newel-post. The house was finished in 1892, just in time to play host to the wedding of the Kelloggs' oldest daughter, Mabel, to banker James Elder. For the next eight decades someone from the Elder family inhabited or owned Number 314.

"It was a gay and happy place, all right," says Adelia Elder Franklin who, like two of her brothers, was born in the house, and who has known Wilfred Cobb all her life. Now seventy-five and a widow, Adelia Franklin lives in an Albuquerque mobile home. It has been several years since she has been in 314, but recollections of it and the special role it played in her life and in others, are vivid. "Downstairs was a large family room, a parlor, a dining room, and kitchen. Upstairs, four bedrooms. Compared to now, it was a pretty unsophisticated place. We had no electricity, and I was seven or eight when the sewer finally came in."

"I came by here now and then as a kid," says Wilfred Cobb. "But back then, this wasn't my sort of neighborhood." If Wilfred Cobb *had* been invited in, he would have seen the two big downstairs fireplaces blazing in the cold months. Under the family piano, which never seemed to remain silent, he would have found Adelia Elder cutting paper dolls. In the kitchen, on Sunday evenings, Cobb might have discovered Adelia's mother making plate-sized pancakes.

Arno Street, which stayed unpaved until about 1920, served as a playground for Adelia, her brothers, and occasionally Wilfred Cobb. "We'd play cops and robbers," Mrs. Franklin says. "Now they do it for real there." One of the first cars on the block was James Elder's 1916 Dodge. In 1925, Adelia and her husband, George Franklin, became parents of a girl, Lila. Because her mother and father frequently were away on business (George Franklin was an FBI-man), Lila Franklin spent a good deal of her youth in Number 314. "Oh, I have such fond thoughts," she says. "One room upstairs had a large victrola. I learned about opera there; there was always music in that house." Today, just about the only music heard in Number 314 comes from Wilfred Cobb's battered bedside radio. "Late at night," Cobb says, twisting his radio's dials, "I like to listen to that Los Angeles station. It comes in real clear."

The 1940s were years of observance and change for the house. In 1942, James and Mabel Elder celebrated their fiftieth wedding anniversary in an elegant parlor Wilfred Cobb now calls home. Four years later, James died at eighty in an upstairs bedroom. (Eighteen years before, his father-in-law, Martin Kellogg, had died in the same room.) In the mid-1940s, when Lila Franklin wed Ned Ross, a clergyman, the couple lived briefly at 314 with *their* infant daughter, Lynn Dee.

Shortly after World War II, just as Wilfred Cobb was receiving a Navy discharge, the family decided to remodel the house. "It was a major job," remembers Adelia Franklin. "We installed all new wiring. We put plumbing in upstairs. We put in new pine floors and stucco over the bricks outside." The biggest transformation, however, was the carving up of the home into four apartments. The family continued to live there, renting out some of those apartments. But Mabel Kellogg's death in 1956 seemed to signal an end. The family was scattered now; no member wanted to live at 314 nor have much to do with it.

For a while, Adelia and George Franklin hired a real estate firm to operate the apartments. For a couple of years a manager lived on the premises and ran the place. In 1965, after much anguish, the Elder-Franklin-Ross family decided to sell the house. By now, old homes on Arno Street were deteriorating rapidly. Renovation had not yet become fashionable. And crime had begun to seep into the neighborhood. Number 314 was sold for $16,000. But the buyers defaulted and the family had to take the house back. That same year, after years of bouncing about various Albuquerque rooming houses, Wilfred Cobb moved into 314.

Never married, Cobb has been a mechanic, carpenter, and a laborer. Though he is the grandson of Edmund G. Ross, a United States senator and later a territorial governor of New Mexico, Cobb has been out of work and drawing Social Security since the early 1960s. His monthly check is $164. Not long after he moved in, Cobb began making repairs. He put up dry wall, fixed broken windows, mended the back fence. In recent years, arthritis and failing eyesight have kept him from doing much. Because of Cobb's loyalty though, the owner-family has never charged him rent. Cobb has never been able to make this work to his advantage. "I've got two dollars to my name now," he says with a snaggletooth smile.

Money doesn't interest Cobb. People do. When he isn't resting on his tiny cot between his two cats, Cobb can usually be found befriending a neighbor. "I don't know what people around here would do without him," says Mrs. John Seth, a widow who lives two houses down. "Mr. Cobb watches my house when he can, he does odd jobs for a lot of people. Once he even chased away a burglar. And he'll never accept payment for anything he does." Mrs. Seth says Cobb is *too* kind. "He buys groceries but they're gone in a couple of days; he gives away everything, mostly to people on welfare."

In the last few years 314 has been home for a steady stream of transients, some worthy, some not. "Couple of alcoholics rented here," Cobb says. "One fellow fell asleep and the sofa caught fire. Nearly burned the house down." It was Cobb who put out that fire to save the building. For all that concern, Cobb will soon be leaving 314. The house has been sold again—this time for $36,000. An eviction notice says all present occupants must vacate within two weeks. Handling the sale was Lila Ross's daughter, Lynn Dee Kelly. Lynn Dee and her husband, Jeff, are real estate agents. "It's not certain exactly what the new owners will do with the house," says Jeff Kelly. "They've talked about living in it while they restore it. How much they'll fix it up, I don't know. No matter what they do, it's going to take a lot of work."

It saddens Lila Ross to think someone from her family, or even Wilfred Cobb, will not have a tie to the house. "You can't believe the sentimental attachment of that place," she says. Had her family been able to afford it, Mrs. Ross would have gladly fixed up the house herself. "Though the only way I would really want it would be as before, like when I was a little girl. And you just can't have it that way." Mrs. Ross's mother, Adelia Franklin, is trying not to let the sale upset her. "You can't go back in time," she snaps. "Selling was a business proposition." But then, "I do hope whoever buys it takes care of it."

Wilfred Cobb, like the other three current tenants in 314, has no firm plans for the future. "Everybody says they're looking around for a little place for me to live," Cobb says. "Sure it'd be nice if the new owners let me stay on here, but that won't happen. Who wants an old man like me around? This house is for young people. People who are going someplace."

This piece provoked several letters. Some correspondents offered apartments; others donated money. Eventually Cobb found a room across town and with the help of Lila Ross, he paid the rent every month. Whenever Cobb got lonely he'd walk two miles to visit his old place. In time, the new owners were gone, and Cobb was back—in Number 314. In January 1982, two years after his return, Cobb was struck and killed by a bus a half block from his home.

Chasing the Cure

ALBUQUERQUE—They were called "lung-ers," but with sympathy rather than derision. Nobody knows exactly when the first lung-er came to Albuquerque. Certainly before New Mexico entered statehood, most likely as early as 1880, when tuberculosis also went by the name "consumption." The teens, twenties and thirties were peak decades for lung-ers. In great numbers they arrived, seeking the high dry air to heal broken breathing tissue, "chasing the cure" doctors around the world said Albuquerque offered.

Almost every day one could spot lung-ers departing a train at the Santa Fe Railway depot. A lung-er hacked loudly, and usually carried only a ratty satchel. His gaunt face wore an alarming look and for good reason: a TB patient's future was not bright. At one time, Albuquerque has as many as six tuberculosis sanatoria, or treatment centers, and perhaps one-fifth of the city's population was made up of people who had come for the cure. Surely the most celebrated lung-er was the late Clinton P. Anderson. A wasted young man when he landed in Albuquerque in

1917 from South Dakota, Anderson got well and went on to become a United States senator and secretary of agriculture.

Others were not so fortunate. Once upon a time tuberculosis was the White Death, a plague like no other this country has known. The fear attached to TB fifty years ago was like the dread that cancer brings today. Thanks to sulfa drugs, vaccines, and antibiotics, tuberculosis, at least in Albuquerque, is rare. What is left are memories. Here are accounts from two survivors remembering their illness and its effect on their lives.

Don Dickason:

I learned of my condition shortly before Christmas 1930. It's not much of a Christmas knowing you have tuberculosis. At the time, I was practicing law in Okmulgee, Oklahoma. That's *O-k-m-u-l-g-e-e*. My hometown was Okemah, Oklahoma. That's *O-k-e-m-a-h*.

I'd been with the Cochran and Noble firm in Okmulgee for a year and a half when I began raising sputum and mucus. Mr. Noble recognized my symptoms right away. "Sounds to me like you've got TB," he said. His niece had had TB. She'd come to Albuquerque and made a recovery and so that's where I went.

All I knew about Albuquerque was that it had this wonderful sunshiny climate. When I got here on New Year's Day, 1931, there was snow everywhere. Cows were hunched up with their tails to the wind. And the streets were slick and icy. I wondered what the hurry was to get here.

The following day I saw Dr. C. C. Davis, the man who treated Mr. Noble's niece. "Both your lungs are infected," Dr. Davis told me. One lung, he said, was "honeycombed." "What's that mean?" I asked. "It means it's not good," the doc said. How serious was TB back then? It was knowing you might not wake up one morning.

Arrangements were made for me to go to the Methodist Sanatorium on Central Avenue. The San had two main buildings with cottages in the middle. Mine was Cottage A. They put me on the "rest cure." That's where you did no activity except go to the bathroom. All your meals were brought in. A nurse would stop by three times a day to see if you were alive.

It was pretty rough for a young man of twenty-four to get used to. I'd been in athletics in school. Once in a track meet in Okfuskee County, Oklahoma, that's *O-k-f-u-s-k-e-e,* I scored thirty-two points. Now I had to rest twenty-four hours. When you're in bed or on a sleeping porch, there isn't much to do. From my windows all I could see were the ambulances that drove up to take someone away to die. That made a believer out of me.

I chased the cure diligently. I didn't play croquet as some of the fellows did, or even join in the nightly pinochle games. Just tended to the business of getting well. I saw too many other people who were back in the San for a second or third time. You see, TB was a disease you had to respect. It was also about the cheapest disease you could have, from the standpoint of treatment. Sixty dollars a month it cost me to stay in the San. And dollars were big as wagon wheels back then.

Doctors considered you were getting well if you started gaining weight. When I checked into the San I weighed 130 pounds. Eight months later I was up to 190. My hat and shoes were too tight to get on. One afternoon Dr. Davis came into my cottage. "You can take exercise now," he said. That meant I could walk five minutes one day, six the next, and so on. I walked all over Albuquerque's East Mesa, which was then just a lizard patch.

In time I recovered enough to go back to Oklahoma. But I started running a fever soon as I got there. Came right back and moved into a rooming house here. There were lots of those kinds of facilities then. TB was Albuquerque's principal industry. I stayed in the rooming house and studied for the New Mexico bar exam, which I took in August of 1931. Scored well enough to be offered a position with the Rodey law firm in Albuquerque. I'm still with it, though don't do much. We've got forty-four other lawyers here. I served in the State Senate three different times and got a number of bills through. I was active in community affairs too. I was so busy I didn't get married till I was thirty-seven.

Yes, I suppose you could say it was a good thing I came here. Now, of course, they use drugs to fight TB. Instead of sending people to New Mexico, they keep them in Oklahoma. They don't attribute climate to the cure anymore. Still, after I saw I wasn't going to be hauled away in an ambulance, I got a better outlook on life. I thought I could make it anywhere and I did.

One incident might interest you. When I entered the San I had a pack of Lucky Strikes in my shirt pocket. When I put back on that shirt eight months later, the pack was still there. I haven't smoked a cigarette since.

Virginie Dinkle:

How did I come to Albuquerque? You're not going to believe this, but I came by ship. For three years I had been living in New York City where I worked in advertising. I had gone to New York as a young girl from my hometown of Kansas City. In the summer of 1934 I started coughing.

"I feel exhausted all the time," I told my New York doctor. "You have tuberculosis, young lady," he said. I had an idea that's what it might be. Two of my older brothers had died of TB.

My doctor recommended I go to Saranac Lake in upstate New York, where there was a large, well-known sanatorium. I wanted to go someplace warmer. So here's what

I did. I took a boat from New York to Galveston, Texas. From there I took a train to Belen, New Mexico. It was cheap; no one had any money then.

It was midnight when I got off the train. To say I was frightened would be an understatement. It was traumatic. I was twenty-two, and alone, and sick.

Right away I went to see Dr. LeRoy Peters, a leading chest specialist. He was on vacation so I saw Dr. Mulky, his associate. I fell in love with Dr. Mulky; he reminded me of the groom on a wedding cake. Dr. Mulky put me into St. Joseph Sanatorium on Grand Avenue, where there were close to 100 patients. I shared a cabin, but had my own bedroom and porch where you sat to get fresh air—and dust.

It was artificial pneumothorax treatment that Dr. Mulky put me on. You must understand this was before they used drugs. In pneumothorax, they injected your pleural area with purified air. They used a long needle that looked to me like a knitting needle. The idea was to flatten the lung and give it a rest.

I was in bad shape. I had five cavities in one lung, three in the other. When my New York doctor wrote to Dr. Mulky asking how he knew which lung to begin on, Dr. Mulky wrote back, "I tossed a nickel." I had so many adhesions the top part of my right lung was completely gone. Pneumothroax was painful. I suppose I cringed each time they arrived in my cabin with the needle, which they brought in a little wooden box.

My roommate in the San was Gerda Hale. She'd been a legal stenographer. She was matter-of-fact, even a bit profane. She was also a strong influence on my life. Over and over she'd say, "Stop feeling sorry for yourself." So I did. We got out of the San together only Gerda died shortly afterward. It was hard for me to take for she was a good friend.

The Sisters of Charity, who ran the San, didn't allow a patient to move around much. What did I do? A great deal of reading. I read *Don Quixote* in French, which took me nearly a year. And I sat in "chase" chairs, which faced the sun. Christmas Day, 1934, was a day I'll never forget. Dr. Mulky came around to see me. "Ginny," he said, "I think Santa Claus has hung a cure on your Christmas tree."

I stayed in the San until May 1935 and then went to a convalescing home on High Street. While there another roomer invited me to the Albuquerque Little Theatre one night. Backstage I met the young man who was starring in *Reunion in Venice*. Clifford Eugene Dinkle was his name, but everybody called him "Tip." He worked for the Albuquerque National Bank, from which he recently retired as senior vice-president. Tip and I were married in 1937.

Twenty years after I got out of the San a second bout with TB sent me back into the hospital. This time I went to Presbyterian Hospital. It was about the only place in Albuquerque that still worked with TB patients. I had seven ribs removed.

If anything, fighting TB toughened me for the hardships that life brings. Our daughter Susan contracted polio in the early 1950s. Our son Steve was sick for six years with a kidney infection. He died in 1967. He was twenty-five.

I'm not a religious person, but at one time if someone said you had TB it was a pronouncement of death. I was put in Cabin Seven. Is that lucky? Or is it something else? I didn't die, I lived. I'm one of those who made it.

Christmas Story

ESCOBOSA—This is a story about a man, his daughter, and some burros. It is also a Christmas story, for the man is kind and whiskered, like a Wise Man; the daughter, all innocence, has a name that evokes the Christ child's; and the burros are not unlike the one Mary rode into Bethlehem. What makes this a Christmas story most of all is that it shows no other season provides a greater understanding of the human spirit.

Paul Marianetti is a big-hearted, big-bearded, middle-aged fellow. Paul works in the City of Albuquerque's accounting department. Until three years ago Paul was married. Then one Christmas his wife asked for a divorce. "She wanted to go her own way," says Paul, who was filled with great bitterness long after. The following Christmas only served to heighten Paul's resentment toward the holiday. His ex-wife and their only child, a seven-year-old girl named Christina, moved from Albuquerque. They went to live in Washington State.

Now, Christina Marianetti, a shy, dark-eyed youngster with skin like a porcelain doll's, means the world to her father. "Little Buzzard," he calls her affectionately. To not have custody of Little Buzzard hurt. "It hurt like hell," Paul says.

Paul sought solace for his pain. His peace came from the 150 acres of Currier & Ives-like land he bought near the Manzano Mountains village of Escobosa, an hour's drive southeast of Albuquerque. Paul cleared a road into the remote area. He built a cabin. He put up barbed wire fences. Though he didn't know much about animals, he bought some cattle and horses. He became a weekend rancher.

For six weeks each summer and at Christmastime, Christina would come to live on the ranch. She would take long hikes with her father on the property that stretches with juniper and ponderosa. She would help with the chores, gather firewood, and feed the animals. At night Christina and her father would toast marshmallows outside over a stone pit.

Between his daughter's visits, Paul read a newspaper article that told how the Bureau of Land Management had an adoption program for wild horses and burros. Always searching for ways to entertain Christina, Paul applied. He asked for a burro. Burros have always meant something special to Paul. When he was little he used to listen to his grandfather, once a poor peddler in Italy, tell of using a burro to pull a wagon loaded with pots and pans. *Il micio* was the old man's endearment for the animal.

A few months after Paul applied, the BLM phoned to ask if he was still interested in adopting. A jenny, or female burro, was available. Someone had previously owned the animal, the BLM said. The burro had been treated cruelly; it needed a new home. Early one Saturday, Paul and Christina, who was visiting, drove to Las Cruces to get the jenny and bring her to Escobosa. All Paul had to pay was one dollar and twenty-five cents for medical shots. It appeared no bargain, however. The burro was skinny and sickly. Its coat was shedding. This bothered Christina not at all. Christina took one glance at the forlorn-looking animal and announced she would be called "Lady Long Ears."

Wild burros can be mean, even ones slightly domesticated. Without warning their hind legs may strike with a furious kick that can send an adult sprawling. A burro's elongated teeth can produce a nasty bite. And should a human show a burro fear, the burro will always be one up.

Christina refused to keep her distance from Lady Long Ears. All over the Escobosa ranch the two romped. "She'd get right up on that burro's back," says Paul. "They really got along well. Everything was perfect." Until Christmas.

A bitter, snowy night in December sent Paul to the ranch. The bad winter weather had forced him to relocate his stock to a safer, more accessible spot on Albuquerque's West Mesa. On his final trip to Escobosa Paul planned to round up Lady Long Ears. He couldn't find her. He searched everywhere, but there was no sign of the burro. While Christina waited in the truck, Paul trudged about the ranch for an hour. Finally, he spotted the little jenny. She was slumped in a bloodied snowbank. Her body had been torn to shreds by a pack of wild dogs. Paul did not have the courage to tell Christina of Lady Long Ears's death. Instead, he lied. He said he couldn't find her.

With tears in his eyes, Paul began the drive back to Albuquerque. On the way he passed the tiny Escobosa Catholic Church. A Christmas candlelight procession was in progress outside. Paul pulled his truck over and watched. Raised a Catholic, it had been years since he had been inside a church, years since his faith meant anything. The divorce and series of unhappy Christmases, including this current one, had left him spiritually numb.

As he studied the faithful filing into the small brick

building Paul was struck by something. "That I had a lot to be thankful for. My family was healthy. I was healthy. I had a good job, a ranch." Suddenly Paul felt ashamed. In all his anger and bitterness he had forgotten about God. But God had not forgotten about him. "I knew," says Paul, "that I had to stop feeling sorry for myself."

Eventually Paul told Christina about Lady Long Ears. As expected, Christina wept. Though torn, Paul applied for another burro. It might help Christina forget, he thought. In August of 1979 the BLM told Paul some burros were available. Christina was in Albuquerque at the time and so accompanied her father again, this time to Arizona. To cushion himself Paul brought home *two* jennies, and a jackass.

This time Paul built a corral around the new burros. The jackass escaped anyway, even before Christina could name him. The animal is called "Houdini" and he still roams somewhere on Paul's ranch. Of the two jennies, Christina named a black one with a broken tooth, "Jenny." The other, who has a silver and dark dorsal stripe, something like a giraffe's, Christina calls "Lady Long Legs."

From the first it was Lady Long Legs who captivated Christina. But try as she might Christina could not mount the animal. The burro refused to be ridden. Paul's daughter left Escobosa that summer without one ride. Christina would be back at Christmas. More than anything Paul felt he had to get her on that burro. All fall Paul battled Lady Long Legs. Much as he pleaded and cursed, he couldn't get a saddle on her.

It took two swift kicks from Lady Long Legs to finally make Paul remember how he had felt outside the little Escobosa church, how he had discovered God cared for him. "What I had to do," Paul says now, "was show that same concern to Lady Long Legs."

Slowly, painstakingly, Paul worked with the animal. Instead of chasing after her with a vengeance, he walked softly. Instead of shouting at her, he talked comfortingly. The saddle never got on but a trust was born. In October Paul bought an old buckboard and restored it. Soon, Lady Long Legs accepted the wagon's harness and reins. What will all this mean when Christina arrives in New Mexico for Christmas?

For one, she will be able to get her ride—not on top, but behind *il micio,* as her great-grandfather once did. The wagon is Christina's Christmas present. And Christina's father? What does he hope for this Christmas? "I've already received my gift," says Paul. "I've had it all along. I just didn't know it."

7: Dreamers

"One of these days I'm going to finish all this."

He Does It His Way

ALBUQUERQUE—"One of these days," Paul Miller is saying as he scans the confusion in front of him," "one of these days I'm going to finish all of this." Half a century of living has led Paul Miller to feel that rushing gets a body no place fast. This is a man who didn't get married until he was forty-five. Taking one's time, Paul believes, enables one to enjoy the pleasures of life. For Paul, there are three important pleasures: his garden, his house, and his wife, and not necessarily in that order. Order is something Paul Miller often overlooks.

The Garden. Paul Miller is not the type of man who would want a farm in a farming area. His garden, eighty feet by eighty feet, sits on a corner lot in Albuquerque's Northeast Heights. It is a busy neighborhood; buses, cars and schoolchildren ramble by at all hours. But Paul Miller likes things a bit chaotic. He says, with the logic that is his alone, that chaos makes him a better gardener. Marching in his own parade, Paul Miller is a man who is hard to keep step with.

The garden is not an ordinary garden. There are three plantings of corn, eight rows to a planting. There is nearly enough corn to feed Rhode Island. There are apple trees, peach trees, plum trees, apricot trees, English walnut trees, pumpkins, broccoli, squash, carrots, sweet potatoes, cucumbers, and more. People often stop to ask Paul if his garden is some kind of produce market. People ask, for instance, if any of his truckloads of tomatoes is for sale. Some people don't even ask; they jump the garden's big fence and help themselves. Paul can't understand this. He would just as soon give his vegetables away as grow them.

While the garden occupies most of Paul's yard, nearly every remaining inch is taken up by what Paul calls "leftovers." Paul works for Sandia National Laboratories. He is also a contractor who builds homes in his spare time. Paul does this work with his brother, Larry, who also helps Paul with the garden and the house. Paul is a lot like Larry but more like Fred Sanford, the Redd Foxx television caracter. Paul likes to bring things home. Some people would call Paul's finds junk. Paul prefers the term leftovers. Every leftover, Paul feels, has potential. With four weatherbeaten doors Paul plans to build a playhouse for his daughter. One of these days. As he does in his garden, Paul cultivates his leftovers. Some he has are a shopping cart, an oxygen tank, a ten-foot-high stack of railroad ties, a monstrous mound of useless tree bark.

Strangers often stop by Paul's garden to ask him what he is going to do with all his leftovers. Many passersby are especially interested in his half dozen tree stumps. Do you really need *all* those tree stumps? people ask. Sure, says Paul. They have potential.

The House. Last year Paul decided he wanted to redo his house. He bought a simple pueblo-style home in 1965. He has never been happy with the house. But because he has been so busy with other chores, Paul never did anything about it. In the past year he has done a lot to the place.

Paul was never satisfied with his home's flat roof. Because he grew up in Indiana, Paul always wanted a house with a pitched roof. Instead of buying a home that resembled a barn, Paul has decided to shape his one-story house into a barn. It has been slow going. Scaffolding, the kind one sees on the side of skyscrapers, has encircled the house for a year now. For many months, tarpaulins have covered the roof and sides of the house. Nobody knows what color the house is anymore. It's white. Paul says the house will be white again—one of these days.

Paul is a master with tools. He learned carpentry from his father back in Indiana. Though Paul's father taught his son how to build a spiral staircase, Paul couldn't figure a way to put one in this house. Instead, he has built a Swiss chaletlike balcony. The east side of Paul's house faces a nice unobstructed view of the Sandia Mountains. For reasons all his own, Paul did not put his balcony on the east side. He put it on the rear of his house, where it looks down upon a neighbor's backyard.

At the same time Paul is redoing the outside of his house, he is redoing the inside. He has ripped out his garage. He has gutted two bedrooms. He has torn down walls and put up walls. To achieve a pitch in his roof, Paul blasted through the ceiling. Never one to work in spurts, Paul is doing all his remodeling simultaneously. And, he likes to point out, without the aid of a blueprint.

The work has not been without its moments. Once, Paul's brother, Larry, laboring on the second story, stepped through the new roof. Larry's legs drove through the ceiling of the dining room. Nothing much was damaged. Nobody uses the dining room except the Millers' two small children. It is, explains Paul, a "catchall" for their toys. Paul says the disarray and inconvenience doesn't bother him. He says when he was a boy, back in Indiana, he and Larry and their father carved a basement under the family home. They raised the roofbeams and added an attic. They turned an entire side of the house around and pointed it in another direction. And they did all the work simultaneously.

Paul indicates that the second story of his house will be used mostly for storage. Even though the new upstairs will bring an additional 1,000 square feet of living space, even though it will include charming dormer windows and be plumbed and wired, when completed the area will be used for storage. Paul says he needs a place to store his nails.

Nobody has offered to buy Paul Miller's house, though many people have shown interest in his handiwork. The people on his block generally admire Paul for what he is: a peerless do-it-yourselfer. Once, last spring, during a downpour, Paul decided he needed to put up sheets of plywood over exposed eaves on his roof. A reasonable idea, except that it was 2:00 A.M. A strong man, Paul Miller does not hammer lightly, even at 2:00 A.M. As Paul pounded with all his might, a neighbor's sleep-disturbed voice could be heard in the rainy darkness. "Miller!" the voice called loudly, but with a touch of sympathy. "What the hell are you doing?"

The Wife. Cathy Miller is a surprisingly cheerful woman several years younger than her husband. She has been married to Paul for five years. Cathy does a lot of watering in the garden. She does a lot of sidestepping of Paul's leftovers, and helps rearrange his catchalls. Cathy frequently holds a ladder for Paul and on occasion helps him pour concrete. If tolerance could be measured on a scale of one to ten, Cathy Miller, who is eight months pregnant, would rate an eleven.

For a long time Cathy wanted her own garden, a flower garden. Paul said she could have one in their small backyard, under the balcony. But Paul insisted Cathy get better topsoil. Flowers don't grow well in arroyo gravel, Paul said. To eliminate the gravel, Paul dug a five-foot wide hole in the tiny plot of land. He intended to fill the hole with topsoil. The hole is still there.

Last summer, during a rainy spell, Paul cut two large sections out of the roof. Cathy says this was a particularly frenzied period. While he was nailing sheetrock overhead, Cathy was scurrying about down below, emptying tubs of rain water.

Cathy dreams of having her living room look like a living room. At the moment it is jammed with packing boxes, a quilting board, tools, leftovers, and Paul's clock collection. In his spare time, Paul builds clocks. Paul always wanted a little mantle clock and so recently he built one. Trouble is, the Millers no longer have a mantle. Cathy has been promised that one of these days, maybe even by next winter, Paul will reconstruct the fireplace he had to remove.

Cathy says she is preparing herself for the day the kitchen is to be demolished. But something worries her even more: Paul has begun to talk about switching around all the bathrooms. Cathy is thankful she still has the master bedroom intact. Even if it is, like the dining room, referred to by the Millers as a catchall. Hanging three feet from the floor in the catchall master bedroom is an elk's head, one of Paul's hunting trophies. Cathy says she still gets frightened when she wakes up in the middle of the night.

Cathy's mother often comes by to visit. When she does, she often shakes her head. She tells her daughter that Paul should have sold the garden and the house long ago and bought such and such a kind of place. Cathy says her mother just doesn't understand Paul; her mother just isn't patient enough. Cathy says Paul's intentions are good. He is a good provider, a good husband, a good father. If Paul seems a little off-center, it might be, suggests Cathy, because the rest of the world is lopsided.

Paul Miller is a man who tends to slip into philosophical musings. For instance, he likes to talk about how much he enjoys hunting. He likes to hunt, he muses, as much as anything in life; it is something he does in his spare time. In the same breath, and with a rationale that is solely his, Paul muses that the fishing isn't all that great in New Mexico. He says he might move to some place where the fishing is better. He says he might even move back to Indiana—one of these days.

Smitty's Bridge

CLOUDCROFT—Heading east up U.S. 82 from Alamogordo, you can see it on your right, down in a canyon. Its shape is a lazy L. Its color, a weatherworn gray. Silent it stands, except on windy days when its boards have been known to groan. Oh, if this bridge could only talk. The Big Trestle, they call it. It's become New Mexico's version of one of the oldest con games: bought and sold in barrooms nearly as many times as the Brooklyn Bridge.

Our tale begins just before the turn of the century in the little town of Cloudcroft, twenty-six miles east of Alamogordo. Perched at a scenic 9,000 feet, Cloudcroft has long been a resort center. Once there was a great deal of logging in the region. To haul the wood out of the Sacramento Mountains, a railroad spur was planned from Alamogordo, where another rail line would run to El Paso, eighty miles to the south. Surveying began in 1897. The railway—the Alamagordo and Sacramento Mountain—finally reached Cloudcroft two years later. The A&SM soon discovered a bonus: it could cater to the lumber boom and bring in vacationers, too. On weekends, El Paso socialites would pay three dollars for a round trip to spend a few days at the Cloudcroft Lodge, a newly constructed, plush hostelry. Though it has burned down once, and been moved, the Lodge survives.

Because the train made more than half a dozen stops, and because the uphill grade at times was nine percent, the trip from Alamogordo to Cloudcroft took over two hours. This was, after all, the highest standard gauge railroad in the world. There were 330 turns, including hairpin and horseshoe curves and corkscrews, zigzags, and a dramatic switchback. Most of the work on the railway was done by Mexican laborers. To traverse the steep chasms, bridges were built. That task went to skilled carpenters from Europe.

More than 100 trestles were constructed, most 100 feet in length or less. The wood used was top-grade red fir, carted in from California. The showpieces were five large trestles. They were marvelous sights: spiderwebs of trusses and hog-jaw braces and tiny guardrails to keep a train from spilling. When a tourist sat in one of the open-sided, yellow excursion cars, and travelled over a large trestle, it was a breathtaking—and very often—frightening experience.

Hundreds of thousands of persons took the "Cloud Climbing Route." In 1947, operations ceased. A modern highway—U.S. 82—had now been built from Alamogordo. Logging trucks could do the work of a train. The railway became a needless luxury. Shortly thereafter the steel tracks were ripped out and the grand trestles removed. All except one. This was a behemoth located one-quarter mile west of the Cloudcroft depot. When the train was running, and townspeople heard the engine's whistle, which was always sounded on that great span, they knew the cars would pull into the station in fifteen minutes. The Big Trestle makes a thirty-degree curve. It stands about sixty feet above the canyon's deepest part. It stretches 323 feet and was built in twenty-one sections, ten timbers to a section. It took nearly two weeks to erect.

By most accounts, the Alamogordo Improvement Company, a subsidiary of the railroad, did the work. The land beneath and around the trestle was owned by the Cloudcroft Company, a now-defunct development firm. In 1917, the railroad acquired an easement from that outfit. Over the next few decades, ownership went back and forth between the railroad, which changed names several times, and the Cloudcroft Company. To complicate matters, the Forest Service acquired the land surrounding the trestle Forest tracts in the area since territorial days. In 1942, the Forest Service acquired the land surrounding the trestle from the Cloudcroft Company. One might assume, then, that the bridge would obviously belong to the government. One should assume nothing, especially if one listens to a supersonic-speaking, chain-smoking, fun-loving Arab named Wedad Smith.

Born sixty-two years ago in the now nearly deserted hamlet of Grenville, New Mexico, near Clayton, Wedad Smith is the son of a Lebanese immigrant. "My first name means *Darling* in Arabic," Smith explains, guffawing loudly. "People call me 'Smitty.' Can you understand why?" Smitty came to El Paso in 1947. He wanted to escape northern New Mexico's cold winters. As a teen-ager in Union County, Smitty once dismantled a railroad as part of a summer job. His dream was to go into the demolition and salvage business in Texas. He's made his goal. And along the way Smitty's sold septic tanks and herded goats. And he's become by his own estimation, a hustler—"without morals, ethics, or bond," as his business card states. His office is his hip pocket. "I may not know everybody in El Paso," says Smitty, horselaughing again. "But by God, I have something on just about everybody."

Sometime, along about the early 1950s, Smitty was

hustling in Cloudcroft. When Smitty plies his trade, he often does it in a local tavern. He was hoisting a few when he says he met one Harry Weaver, a San Angelo, Texas, architect. "Old Harry," says Smitty, lighting another Salem, "he said he'd sell me four trestles on the railroad. I bought 'em. Figured I could sell the materials." According to Smitty, Weaver said he had bought the trestles from someone named Irwin Schwartz, or a lumber company; Smitty can't remember which. Nor will Smitty reveal how much he paid Weaver. He does indicate it came to about $3,000 a trestle. "If I told you the exact amount," Smitty booms, "the tax man would be all over me."

When Smitty went to study his purchases, he noticed that the Big Trestle would be a problem to remove. Little Mexican Canyon, where it sits, is precipitous. There was no access road. The job would be hazardous. And while the bridge's twelve-inch by twelve-inch vertical supports were prime goods, there was nothing Smitty could do. "That's when I went to the Lincoln National Forest's supervisor and verbally gave him the trestle," Smitty recalls. "But it was still mine, see."

It took Smitty nearly ten years to tear down the other three trestles. He'd drive up on weekends from El Paso or wherever he happened to have a hustle going. Using giant motorized pliers, Smitty would carefully squeeze one of the wooden structures like an accordion. Then he'd drop it like a deck of cards. Then he'd use a winch to pull out the pieces. Smitty never used explosives on the trestles, and he worked solo. Only once did Smitty bring his wife up to help. It was such a disastrous experience it led him to create this rule: "Never let your wench run your winch."

Meanwhile, the Big Trestle went unmolested. In time, people began to identify the bridge with the town. Artistic reproductions, including a painting by former area resident Bill Maudlin, the cartoonist, were churned out. Ashtrays, lithographs, pottery, post cards, wall hangings, and T-shirts featured the structure. The Cloudcroft Chamber of Commerce had itself a symbol. Still, no one was completely sure who owned it. This became evident in 1964 when a Holloman Air Force Base enlisted man named Larry Swanke dropped by the Otero County clerk's office in Alamogordo with a fistful of money. Swanke explained how someone—and he didn't remember exactly who—had told him the trestle could be his if he paid some taxes on it. Swanke made some payments, then decided the whole thing was more trouble than it was worth. After that, strangers began to appear regularly in Cloudcroft real estate offices to make bids on the bridge. By the mid-1960s, those interested in preserving Cloudcroft's past sensed that while it was probably good business to have the trestle etched on a beer stein, it probably was not such a great thing to have people running around saying they owned the darn thing. Something had to be done.

The first step toward legitimation came in 1968. The town got the Forest Service to widen the highway near the trestle, so that passersby might get out of their automobiles and take pictures without being run over. A year later, the State Highway Department, through the urgings of Cloudcrofters, added an authoritative roadside marker that tells the story of the mountain railway. There was talk about making the trestle a National Park Service historic landmark, but that never came about. In 1970, however, the bridge was entered on the New Mexico Register of Cultural Properties. While these actions did help to deter vandalism and give the trestle credibility, they did not completely curtail ownership claims.

The most fervent assertion came in the late 1970s. An El Paso trucking executive named Albert Coca turned up to say he had bought the Big Trestle from another El Pasoan, attorney Frank Owen. A check of the Otero County clerk's files showed a bill of sale between the two men, but no record of how the trestle came to Owen. Never mind, Coca told Cloudcroft village officials, the trestle was his. And Coca said if he didn't get $10,000 for it within a couple of days, he was going to dispatch one of his truck crews to New Mexico, with orders to rip down the huge edifice.

That threat threw Cloudcroft into a dither. History buffs howled. The Forest Service bristled. Old-timers, like John Mershon, a state representative from the area, scratched their heads in disbelief. Mershon, whose home and office were just up the road apiece from the trestle, says now, "The whole thing had the odor of blackmail."

Initially, the Otero County assessor's office said if Coca *really* wanted the trestle, he'd have to pay $13,000 in back taxes to get it. That response only opened the wound further. Finally, Department of Agriculture attorneys were called in. What they found was a jurisprudent jungle of rights-of-way, doctrines of adverse possessions, and absolutely no legal precedents. Federal lawyers eventually agreed that the trestle was abandoned by the railroad in 1948, and thus could have been sold to other parties. But legally, the opinion stated, the Forest Service, which took over the easement in 1942, along with any future abandonments, owned the bridge—lock, stock, and three-quarter inch bolts.

Albert Coca then received a threat of his own: should he so much as loosen a splinter of the trestle, criminal charges would be filed by the U.S. government. Wisely, Coca backed off. Coca refuses to speak about the affair, but Frank Owen did talk by telephone from El Paso. "I do remember it [the sale] being a pretty casual thing. There was no big mystery about it. I bought the trestle from a friend who bought it from a friend of his. The thing is, I can't remember the name of either of those fellows. But I'm sure it's all on file somewhere." Owen added that he paid $2,000 for the trestle, and that Coca paid him about the same. "It was done in good faith," Owen said.

Such pronouncements tend to make Wedad Smith laugh more than usual. Smitty has known Owen and Coca for a number of years. Their transaction has a familiar ring to it. "Those boys," confirms Smitty with a roar, "occasionally drink at the same bars as I do." Smitty believes the Big Trestle is rightfully his. Yet Smitty's bill of sale cannot be found in the Otero County Courthouse. "Oh, it's there," Smitty argues. "I know. Ask old Harry Weaver." And where is old Harry? "Beats me," says Smitty.

John Mershon, who considered himself a historian for the Cloudcroft area, dismissed the claims of all three El Paso men. "The First National Bank of Artesia owned the trestle," Mershon revealed. "The bank took possession after a man defaulted on a loan he had taken out to buy the structure from the railroad. The man's name was Wilburn, I think. He was from Hope, New Mexico."

The convoluted events described above have not provided much amusement for residents of Cloudcroft. The trestle is, after all, not some used Pontiac whose papers have been misplaced. "I got my doubts anybody owned it but the Forest Service," says James Sewell, Cloudcroft's Kris Kringle-looking mayor for the past thirty years. Sewell also runs the community's Western Bar, where talk often turns to the trestle. "Can't understand all the fuss," continued Sewell. "The timber in that ain't worth much now. It's so full of bullet holes and dry rot that a sawmill would likely tear it up." Still, the trestle means something to Sewell. As a kid, he used to chase chipmunks on it. "I'd like to see it be used again. I'd like to see a little tourist railroad come back here, like the one they got up in Chama. That'll probably never happen, though."

Two years ago, Cloudcroft and the Forest Service worked to get the trestle listed on the National Cultural Register, as further protection. For eighty-five dollars, the town could have gotten a ten-inch by fifteen-inch commemorative bronze plaque to display on a piling. Residents refused to pay. The plaque, they figured, might have been stolen or sold. Except for inspired carvings—"Dave and Cathy;" "Go Bears"—there is nothing now on the trestle. How long the bridge will last is anybody's guess. The original wood was never treated. It's not a rickety framework, but it probably could no longer support the weight of a locomotive. People are surprised to learn they can walk out on the trestle, from the north end. It can't be traversed completely, however. After a small girl fell to her death in the mid-1950s, the south end's bulkhead was removed. "The whole thing's a dangerous headache," says Jim Abbott, Lincoln National Forest supervisor. "If we restore the trestle, then it's not really a historic site. And if there's an accident, then we're liable. At some point we'll just have to fence it, I guess."

Wedad Smith, incorrigible merrymaker, is standing on the trestle. In the distance, to the west, the White Sands shimmer. In Smitty's eye, there is a gleam. "This bridge was precision made," Smitty is telling three camera-toting tourists. "You couldn't get one of these things built today. You couldn't hardly even find anyone who knows how to design one." As the trio of sightseers absorbs this information, Smitty chatters on. "I bet," he says laughing a deep P. T. Barnum laugh, "I bet I could find somebody somewhere who'd give me a thousand bucks for this bridge."

The Long Walk

TAOS—A fall afternoon sun has put a halo over the Taos Elementary School playground. In the center of the field a large group of youngsters is randomly kicking soccer balls. On the sideline, a small, dark-featured man with a crooked nose is watching with a smile. From a distance the man looks like a kid. Indeed, more than one person has remarked that there's a lot of little boy in Jesse Castaneda. "Fantástico!" Jesse shouts. The word, a favored one, comes out *Fun-tas-teee-co*. Turning to a spectator, Jesse reveals that a little girl named Maria has just made a fine kick. Maria wears a leg brace.

After a few more moments Jesse runs onto the field. When he does, a mother of one of the children appears alongside the spectator. The woman explains that before Jesse Castaneda came to Taos a year ago, there was no organized soccer program in the community, and that Taos kids had little to do. "Jesse is such an unselfish person," the mother goes on. "He means everything to us." Then she adds, "We'll be sorry to see him go." And where is Jesse going? Beginning in October 1981, he plans a little stroll, 20,582 miles, give or take a mountain range, from the southernmost tip of South America to the bottom of Alaska—on foot. That's Jesse's dream; some say it's a pipedream, a loco idea, that this time Jesse Castaneda has, well, walked off the deep end.

Enormously generous yet stubbornly idealistic, it's unlikely there has ever been a more curious sports figure in New Mexico than Jesse Castaneda. Part Don Quixote, part Norman Vincent Peale, he is an infectious humanitarian. His humility is exceeded only by enormous pride, mistaken for ego by some. Jesse (irrepressible free spirits like this are seldom called by their last names) has walked more miles over a twenty-four hour period than anyone; you could look it up. He's hobnobbed with the British Parliament and served the dirt poor. An artist with more enthusiasm than talent, all his life Jesse has done things for others. Still, he lives in two tiny rooms and dreams of an outlandish hike that will take three years to complete. What can one make of such a person? "There's nobody quite like Jesse," says a friend. "He's a maverick, yet he's the most upbeat, giving guy on earth."

In the mid-1970s, Jesse Castaneda was nearly as wellknown as anyone in New Mexico. Because he constantly seemed to be setting—or attempting to set—endurance walking records, he made the news regularly. Many of his walks he did for charity. If you had a cause—multiple sclerosis, diabetes, rape crisis, psoriasis even—you summoned Jesse. He'd do a solo number or lead a group—for free. The Albuquerque Sports Hall of Fame voted him Athlete of the Year. He had a good job at the Albuquerque Academy. He had made the *Guinness Book of World Records*. Then the bottom fell out. Some people believe it happened because Jesse became *too* famous. In 1976, his first marriage to a nurse who bore him two daughters, broke up. A year later, another marriage, which also produced a daughter, ended in divorce. In 1978, Jesse was fired by the Academy where he had taught Spanish and physical education for eleven years. The dismissal cited Jesse's "irresponsible behavior," and that he was not "fully committed" to teaching. Being let go hurt Jesse badly. He had shared his celebrity with the school: he had set several of his records on the Academy running track. A lawsuit was filed, later to be dropped.

After the Academy, Jesse took over as director of New Mexico's Council on Physical Fitness. He devised all sorts of offbeat health tests, like nonstop bowling. When a new governor took office, Jesse was relegated to a basement office, and forgotten. Frustrated, he quit that job. In 1979, Jesse left Albuquerque, where he had lived for twenty-five years, and fled to Taos. Albuquerque, he says now, stopped caring for him. Because he wears his feelings on the sleeve of his warmup suit, Jesse is a man who must be loved in return.

Jesse knew no one in Taos, but it didn't take long before everyone knew him. Says his friend Frank McGuire, "If you're within one hundred yards of Jesse, you meet him." Immediately Jesse founded the Taos Youth Soccer League, which now draws 215 youngsters. Organizing soccer programs was nothing new to Jesse. In 1972, he began one in Albuquerque with six kids. That project's grown to 6,000.

Jesse settled in Taos with his third wife, Mary Shorter, sister of marathoner Frank Shorter. The couple and their eighteen-month-old son, Carlos, live a quick sprint from famed Ranchos de Taos Church, in a cramped apartment they rent from Mary's mother. Souvenir Frisbees from various benefit walks hang from one wall of the home. There's a poster of Mary's brother. A makeshift shelf holds two hardbound copies of the *Guinness Book*.

From the Taos soccer venture, Jesse receives only gas and food money. And he must get that by begging local merchants. In the winter months he does odd jobs at the Taos Ski Valley. Mary Castaneda, a reserved, honey-haired woman, works part-time in an art supply store. Times are tough, but the Castanedas are happy. You live with Jesse, says Mary, you become happy. Jesse is after all a member of the Optimist Club. "The only time Jesse gets at all discouraged," says Mary, "is when people don't support him who say they will. That's happened before. I hope it doesn't happen with this walk."

The Walk. Jesse calls it The Walk of the Century. It's been brewing since he came to Taos. Jesse was reading a map of North and South America bird migration when the idea struck. Why not take off like some giant fowl and go from Tierra del Fuego to Anchorage? Long distance walking is nothing new to Jesse. He computes he's walked around the world two and one-half times. He's kicked a soccer ball up the Sandia Mountains' La Luz Trail, but that's another story. The point is, new walking feats are in short supply. Someone has already walked across the United States—backwards, for heaven's sake. What's left? A Pan American perambulation, if you will.

Word on The Walk spread quickly. Just as fast, a few hitches developed. Southwest Sports, a public relations firm Jesse employed, went out of business. That in turn slowed financial backing. Jesse figures that to transport himself, Mary, Carlos, and a backup crew to South America, to feed, clothe, provide vehicles and supplies over three years, will cost a minimum of $300,000. The Taos Soccer League is doing well, but 300 grand is stretching the budget. Then where will the money come from? Vaguely, Jesse mentions shoe companies. "After all," he says, "I will wear out about eighteen pair of running shoes. Adidas should be interested. Maybe Nike." The problem is Jesse has not contacted either firm or any other. Jesse seems unconcerned. "Do you know anybody at the *National Geographic?*" he gaily asks his guest. "They will want to help me, I'm sure."

"You ought to talk to George Maloof," Mary Castaneda tells her husband. (Now deceased, Maloof was a philanthropic Albuquerque businessman.) "Fantástico!" Jesse responds. "I will. Tomorrow." Jesse says that a "board" of persons will help get The Walk in gear. "We will be meeting in December," he confirms. "I think." A television sportscaster has several times promised to do a piece on Jesse. "He was supposed to be up here this morning," says Jesse. "Next week maybe." Lack of interest in The Walk is not as big an obstacle as Jesse's lack of focus; he has yet to explain *why* he is walking. He speaks of "unity of mankind," of "fitness," of "goodwill," of "conservation." That there is no clear-cut reason other than doing something that's never been done before may not be enough. Still, Jesse expects corporate donations to pour in. An Optimist never doubts. Mike Rice, president of the Taos Chamber of Commerce, has been asked to serve on Jesse's "board." Says Rice: "Jesse's got a heart as big as an elephant, but he's no businessman. He needs someone who knows fund-raising to guide him. Right now he doesn't have that person."

Meanwhile, Jesse trains. He puts in ten to twelve miles a day of hard walking. The conditioning takes his mind off the logistics of The Walk. "I never liked paperwork anyway," he says. George Goldstein verifies that. As New Mexico's secretary for Health and Environment, Goldstein worked with Jesse when Jesse was the state's physical fitness chief. "I don't think I ever saw Jesse behind a desk. We had our best conversations when we were exercising." Goldstein thinks the only thing that can stop The Walk is lack of funds. "Jesse's supposed to know the Kennedy family," Goldstein muses. "Maybe they can help him."

Frank McGuire, director of a statewide energy program, has known Jesse twenty years. McGuire is so certain about The Walk that he plans to quit his job and accompany Jesse. "If it were any other person, I wouldn't be so positive." Jesse claims that McGuire may get the Los Alamos Scientific Laboratories to contribute weather studies for The Walk. All of this is to be discussed soon, according to Jesse. "Frank's supposed to be up here next week. Or the week after."

Jesse indicates that Dr. Hemming Atterbom may be a member of The Walk's support crew. Director of the Human Performance Laboratory at the University of New Mexico, Atterbom ran stress tests during several of Jesse's nonstop walking efforts. Once Atterbom even took Jesse to the hospital when he collapsed during a record attempt. When asked about The Walk, Atterbom says, "If Jesse pays for my ticket, I'll go anywhere." Atterbom thinks Jesse would have no physical trouble with the feat. "The things that could stop him are disease, a war, and of course, money. Couldn't he get Kodak to do something for him?"

What makes Jesse Castaneda run—or rather, walk—after such a big dream? One feeling is that Jesse tries harder because he is small. He is five-feet, five inches tall. "Five-six on a good day," he cracks. Frank Papcsy, who first met Jesse two decades ago, doesn't buy the "little man" theory. "I think," says Papcsy, "that if Jesse was twice the size he is he'd be the same person."

Another opinion connects Jesse's drive to his being a foreigner. Jesse has been in this country twenty-five years, but he is not yet an American citizen. He is a Mexican who has embraced Yankee determination. Jesse was born in Agua Prieta, in the state of Sonora, in 1940. Though Agua Prieta has no mountains, Jesse says it resembles Taos in its friendliness. Because he often returns to Agua on mercy missions for the youth of that community, there exists the belief that Jesse grew up in an orphanage. He didn't. His father, now dead, was a travelling salesman for a clothing company. His mother still resides in Agua and is the only person who has strongly urged Jesse not to go on The Walk. "Too dangerous," Lilia Castaneda believes.

His childhood was a happy one, dominated by sports of every kind. "We also played 'chicken'," remembers Jesse, "with moving freight trains." One event provided grit early. At age eight, Jesse was hit by a moving car and was told he'd never walk again. Three months later he was on his feet. He came to the United States at sixteen with the intention of studying agriculture in Amarillo, Texas. When he explained his plans to a customs official at the Arizona border, Jesse was told, "Don't go there, go the the Menaul School." The next thing Jesse knew he was bound for Albuquerque. "I could only speak three words—'Yes,' 'No,' and 'Maybe'." Language would plague him for years. He still has trouble with English past tenses, and certain pronunciations. For instance, the word *journey*, as in "my 20,000-mile journey," emerges as *yur-knee*.

At Menaul, Ruth Barber, the former principal, drilled Jesse relentlessly in speech and grammar. She also decided it would be better for him to be called "Jesse" rather than his given name, "Jesús." Though he weighed 120 pounds, Jesse played football at Menaul. Dave Tomlinson, Menaul's former football coach, gives an example of Jesse's resoluteness. "I saw him get knocked unconscious in a playoff game in Tatum, and I practically had to drag him off the field." Tomlinson, too, recalls Jesse's struggles with English. "Because he didn't always understand directions, he'd wander all over the place when he played defense. It used to drive me up the wall." Nonetheless, Jesse made All-State at guard. "He was," says Tomlinson, "a courageous kid who just never gave up."

By the time he entered the University of New Mexico, Jesse was up to 130 pounds, good enough, he figured, to play college football. Frank Papcsy, professor of physical education at UNM, was Jesse's adviser. Papcsy remembers a Lobo football coach pleading with him to advise Jesse to quit the squad. "But Jesse wouldn't quit," relates Papcsy. "He'd go to practices literally held together by tape. Finally he did quit, but only after he developed other interests." One was soccer. Papcsy served as the UNM soccer coach years back, and he likes to tell the story of how Jesse broke a foot in one game. "Didn't bother him; he just took painkillers. The next day Jesse was out running like nothing happened."

Race walking came along in 1971. Because of his age, Jesse realized he would never be Olympic caliber. Still, walking intrigued him. "It's creative," he says. "When I walk I like to observe things—animals, people, the environment. You can't always do this when you run or jog." Creativity is important to Jesse. A distant relative of writer-philosopher Carlos Castañeda, there is a great deal of the visionary in Jesse. He paints abstracts; he writes poems. There is also some impracticality. Jesse paid a New York vanity press $4,000 to publish two books of smarmy inspirational poetry he'd penned. Yet the books were not ego trips; Jesse did them to share with others an unharnessed *gusto de vivo*. "Jesse's motives have always been laudable," says Hemming Atterbom. "He never does things just for himself. He always has an ulterior reason."

Soccer practice over, Jesse takes his guest to Taos Ski Valley. It seems fitting that Jesse should work here. Ernie Blake, the resort's owner, and the man who hired Jesse, is something of an original himself. Asks Ernie: "How you cannot love Jesse?" Jess does "public relations" for Blake. "I work in the parking lot," he says without embarrassment. It's hard to be creatively benevolent parking cars, yet Jesse found a way. When a drunk Texan made a commotion and threatened to pull a gun in the lot, Jesse, all smiles stepped in. "I just tell him God loves him," Jesse says. "I think it shocks him because he left. You try to see good in everybody."

At Jesse's invitation, the guest follows him up a steep ridge. There is snow underfoot, but no one is skiing yet. In the distance, toward Arizona, the sun is setting. Barely breathing hard, Jesse takes in the view. As he does, he lets loose one more *Fantástico!* Jesse once wrote a poem called *I Can See Forever*. In it he talks of the harmony that fills a man's soul when he is at peace. Since he wrote the poem, Jesse has had some unsettling times. Certain people have stopped believing in him—bosses, friends, and wives. He has forgiven all, and now has peace again. He says complete harmony will come when he begins The Walk. "Winnebago should be interested, don't you think?" Jesse wonders aloud. "After all, we'll be using a big motor home for the *yur-knee*. I want to talk to the people at *Sports Illustrated*. Maybe the *New York Times* . . . Gatorade. . . ."

Though its starting date has twice been postponed for a year, The Walk is still on, according to Jesse. And he says he's found a new source of money for the venture—Caesar's Palace.

Gone Fishin'

NAVAJO DAM—Abe Chavez has heard just about every bad fishing joke. Like fishing being a jerk at one end of the line waiting for a jerk at the other. Abe always laughs anyhow, giving you the feeling that when he stops laughing, he'll stop fishing. And it's pretty hard to imagine Abe Chavez not fishing. Some folks say Abe is a con man, that he makes extravagant claims about the size and surplus of trout in the San Juan River. Abe's a charmer, all right. He sells the San Juan because, like the blood that flows through his veins, the clear, cold river runs near to Abe's heart.

"I love this river," a visitor heard Abe say to some tourists one weekday morning recently at Abe's Tackle Box, thirty-five miles east of Farmington. The tourists had just spent the night at Abe's Motel, and spent the morning putting away a whale-sized platter of scrambled eggs in Abe's Cafe. The tourists now were experiencing the San Juan River's second best attraction: fishlosopher Abe Chavez holding court. "My father taught me to fish this river," Abe is saying. A short, swarthy chatterbox, Abe is a near dead-ringer for professional golfer Lee Trevino. "We were living in Farmington then, the first Mexican family to settle there. My father, also named Abe, was a boxer. He was known as the "Farmington Flash," and was ranked third in the world in the 1930s. Jack Dempsey refereed three of his fights. I boxed some, too; won the New Mexico Golden Gloves in forty-eight, as a bantamweight. Then I got hit by the fishing bug."

The mortar wasn't mixed on Navajo Dam in 1955 when Abe, then twenty-two, arrived at the site with his wife, Patsy, one child, and $300 in fishhooks. Abe wanted to start a sporting goods store, maybe sell some fishing licenses, rent himself out as a guide in the just-opened playground. Abe's businesses grew up almost overnight, like the dam. Today he is almost everything at Navajo Dam, except postmaster; that's Patsy's job.

By the time the tourists leave, enriched by Abe's information in ways not always immediately understood, Abe is ready to get down to the business of fishing. Ten o'clock is not known as the best time of day to test the San Juan, but no matter to Abe. "I got a feeling we're going to catch something big," he tells a visitor while we load up a battered white pickup. After filling up at Abe's Gas Station, and rambling out past Abe's Boat Storage, we find a parking spot alongside a quiet bank of the river. "The biggest mistake amateurs make here is using too big a line—a twelve or an eight is too big," Abe says, baiting a four-pound test. "A trout's a real pro; he can see that heavy line." Abe hooks a minnow for bait.

As Abe's line hits the water, his commentary begins. "The San Juan's a hard river if you're just starting out. But you can get lucky. I like to help beginners, that's what built up my business. Experts here have been good enough to pull in twelve-pound rainbows. My biggest was only seven pounds. Best fisherman I've ever seen is Dr. John Rose, from Albuquerque. He comes up here all the time with his brother and they're always competing, just like my Dad and me used to. You want to know what makes a good fisherman? He's got to read the water, got to move the bait from left to right. Some experts say you should wear dark clothes. Probably wouldn't hurt. Others say you should always be quiet, never talk. Do you really think a fish can understand me? Fishing's like my twin sisters; they used to sing, but every time company would come around they wouldn't."

Making a thirty-yard cast, Abe speaks of the San Juan's citizens—rainbow and German brown trout. "Got to take your time with rainbows; they're showoffs. They'll come near the top, then disappear. German browns, they'll go down by nature, to the weeds. No matter, a trout likes moving bait. Hey, but no fisherman likes to be told something outright. Their grandfather or somebody showed them how long ago. I don't jump up and down with advice; I kind of ease into it. All except tangled lines. I've seen some lines so tangled they couldn't get that bad even if you did it on purpose."

Back in the pickup, Abe takes the visitor to another part of the San Juan. Here the river meanders behind Abe's home. From the back of his truck Abe grabs some waders. "There's been about five people around here killed wearing these," he says of the hip boots. "You fall down in the water, the waders fill up, and you drown pretty quick." Casting rapidly, Abe moves away from death just as quickly. "Bragging's a part of fishing, sure. It's in all of us. It's like teen-agers talking about how much beer they drank." Moving a few steps forward, Abe gets his first strike of the morning. "Right over there," he says, sounding a bit like a hungover teen-ager might, "I got one of the biggest fish you ever say. But he got away." Abe points to a cliff above the visitor's head. "I've stood up there and spotted a fifteen-pound German brown down here. I'll get him some day." Then a final cast, and a final plea: "C'mon, one less of you guys ain't gonna hurt this river."

Empty-handed, we head back to the pickup. On the way we pass a pile of beer cans and soda bottles dumped along one side of the San Juan. Says Abe sadly of the litter, "It's the only thing wrong with this river." There are, of course, many good things about the San Juan. "The fish here are gorged," gushes Abe. "There's plenty to eat. Other rivers have gone bad, but this one has stayed good. It doesn't need any stocking."

Abe's voice carries an edge. Upriver from Abe's Tackle Box a power plant is being proposed at Navajo Dam. The plant would provide irrigation for Navajo farmers' pumps. The environmental threat of such a plant hangs over Abe's river like dark clouds. "The way I look at it," Abe says, "if the plant ruins the river, someone will just say, 'Sorry,' and then what are you going to do about that?" In a few minutes Abe and the visitor arrive at the dam, a monstrosity of human endeavor, 400 feet high. After a quick look, Abe turns around his truck and heads back to the Tackle Box. He is silent for a moment, but only for a moment.

"Religion's what our freedom's based on," Abe says, apropos nothing special. "My father was Protestant, but my mother was Catholic, like ninety-nine percent of the Spanish are. Boy, did they go at each other sometimes. My father and mother, I mean. A lot of people think I'm Jewish. The name *Abie,* I guess. I'm not Jewish, though I got two nephews named Ephraim and Jeremiah. Patsy, she was Catholic until she heard an evangelist in Farmington. Now she's Protestant like me and everything's fine. Patsy's been the reason for my success. She's 'book smart.' We get along even working side by side. No, I never thought about divorce. Oh, maybe murder a few times."

When we reach the Tackle Box, Abe announces he is hungry. Patsy Chavez meets us at the door, amused by her husband's poor luck fishing. Abe has an explanation. "Some of the little ones," he says, laughing, "must have seen us and went and told the big ones." Patsy has prepared a trout dinner, fish she says she caught herself. We take a booth in Abe's Cafe. Between bites Abe says, "I used to get crushed when I didn't catch anything. But you know, the older I get the more I see that you're not going to win everytime out. And you shouldn't. Life's not like that."

The meal over, the visitor follows Abe next door to the Tackle Box where the host starts in on the perils of fish hooks. "Dogs are the worst to take them out of," Abe says. "I've pulled hooks out of people's faces and hands. Until a doctor showed me how, for a long time I used razor blades to remove them. Now I cut the barb first, and then go around it. Ten years ago, Patsy put one in my rear end." Standing nearby, Patsy chuckles at the memory. She has endured her husband's preoccupation for line and lure for years—well, ever since the birth of the couple's first child. Randy Chavez was born while his father was away—fishing.

Customers have begun to fill the Tackle Box. Many are staring at the dozens of snapshots stuck beneath the glass counter tops. Abe is in several of the photos, posing with proud fishermen and their catches. "All sorts of people come here to stay," Abe is saying. "Peter Hurd, the artist, George Peppard, the actor, governors, senators, the editor of *Field & Stream*, the magazine. People are calling from every state, asking how the fishing is. An old guy used to come all the way from Florida to stay with me. When he turned sixty-five, he called up and said, 'Abie, I'm going to get married and spend my honeymoon with you.' I was tickled. I made him up a big cake with a river on the top in icing, and words that said, 'Lord, help me catch a fish.' He was here fifteen days. Can't remember if he caught anything. Do remember he said he had a great time."

Suddenly Abe asks the visitor for the time. As a favor, Abe has promised to take a man and his son fishing that afternoon. Only then does the visitor notice Abe doesn't wear a wristwatch. An unbothered man, his timekeeper is the river. Abe's visitor once knew a bothered man, a fellow named Lyons. If Lyons didn't like someone (and he didn't like most people), he frequently delivered the same sarcastic forecast. "That guy," Lyons would say, "will end up selling fishhooks." Lyons probably never met Abe Chavez, and it's a shame. He would have liked Abe. He might even have bought some fishhooks.

Perhaps it is fitting that this piece concludes the collection. Abe Chavez was one of the first persons I met on my travels across the state. And Abe's outlook on life—singular, uncomplicated, enlightening—says to me as much about New Mexico as anyone's.